Thes Coloring Book belongs to

_____

_____

_____

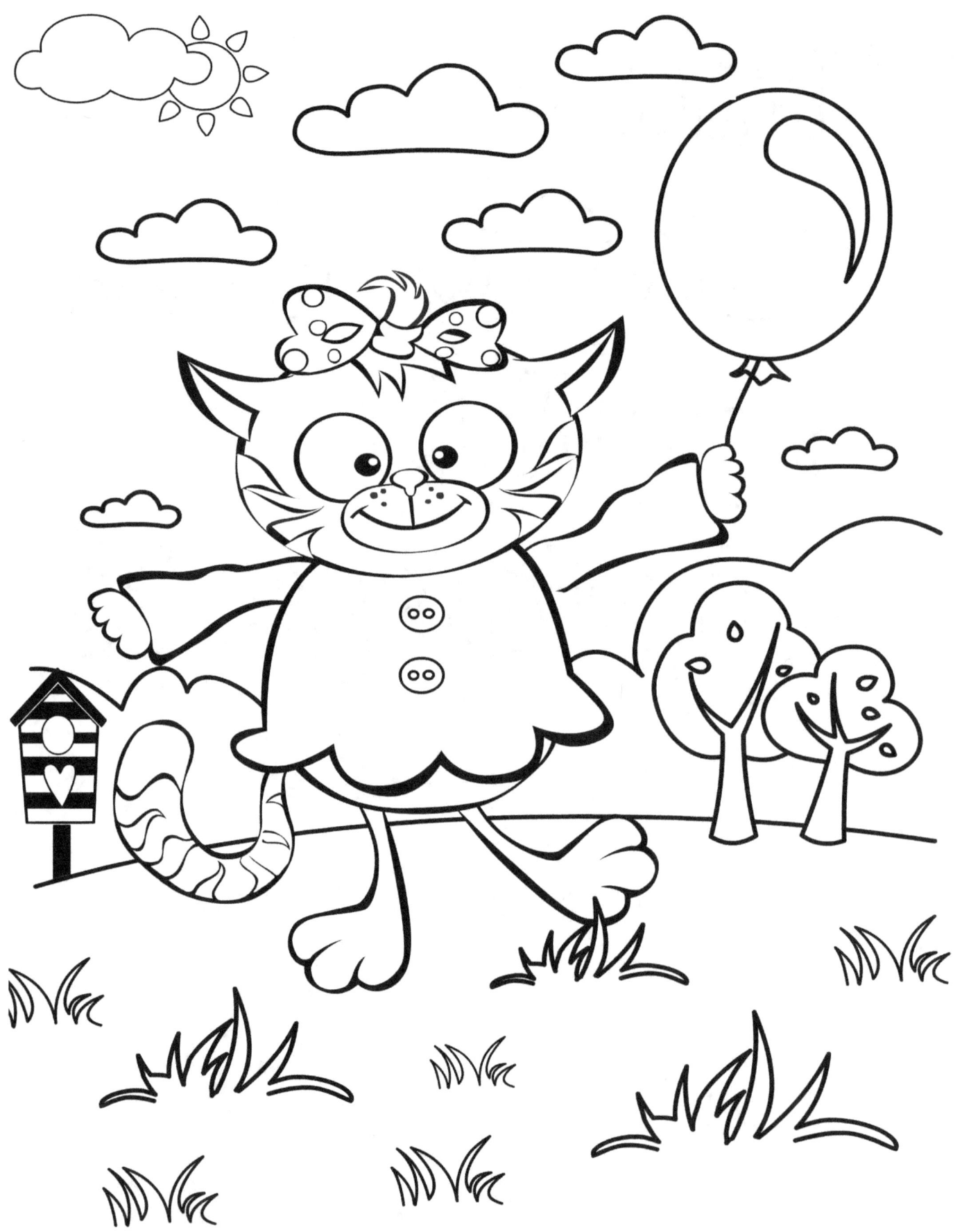

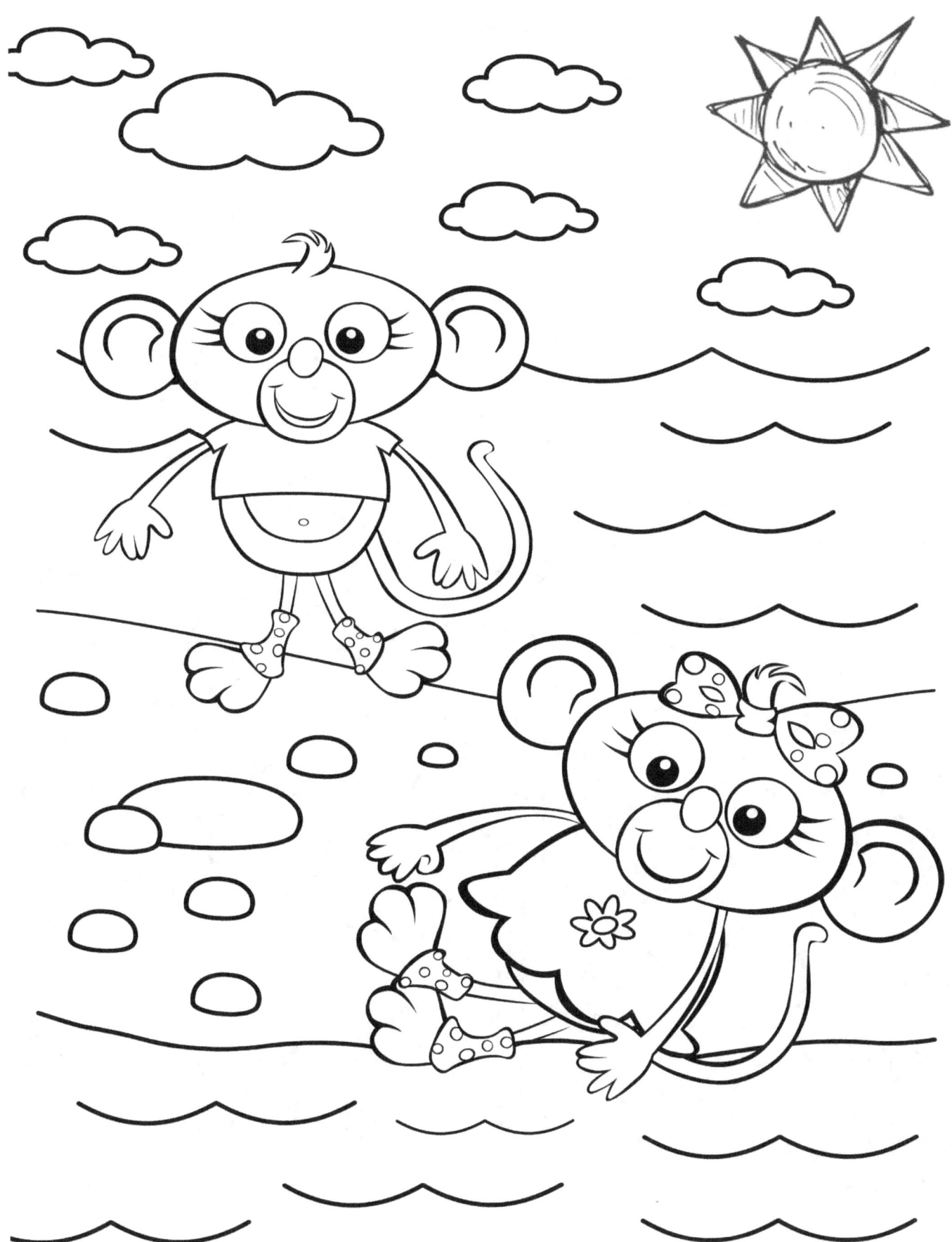

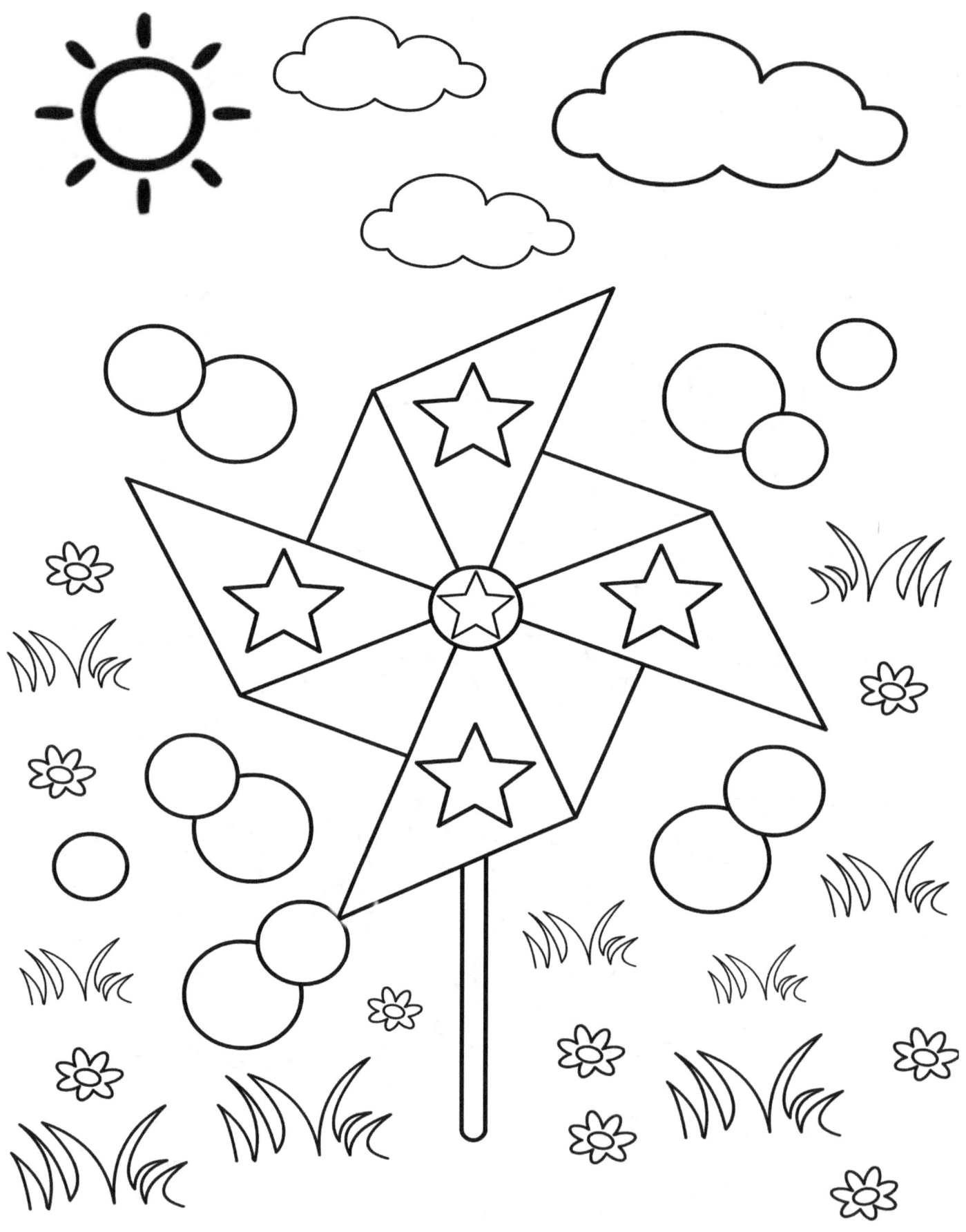

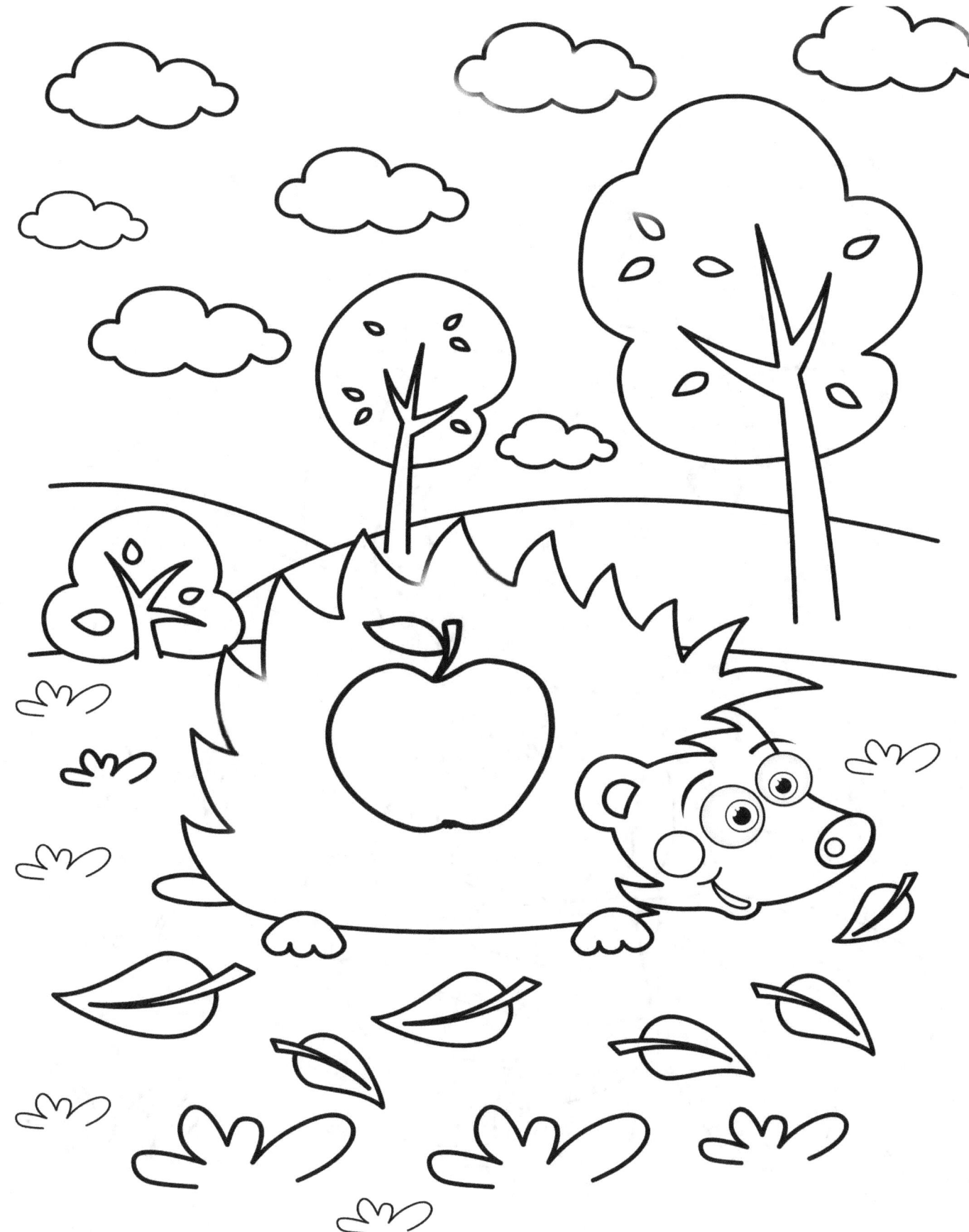

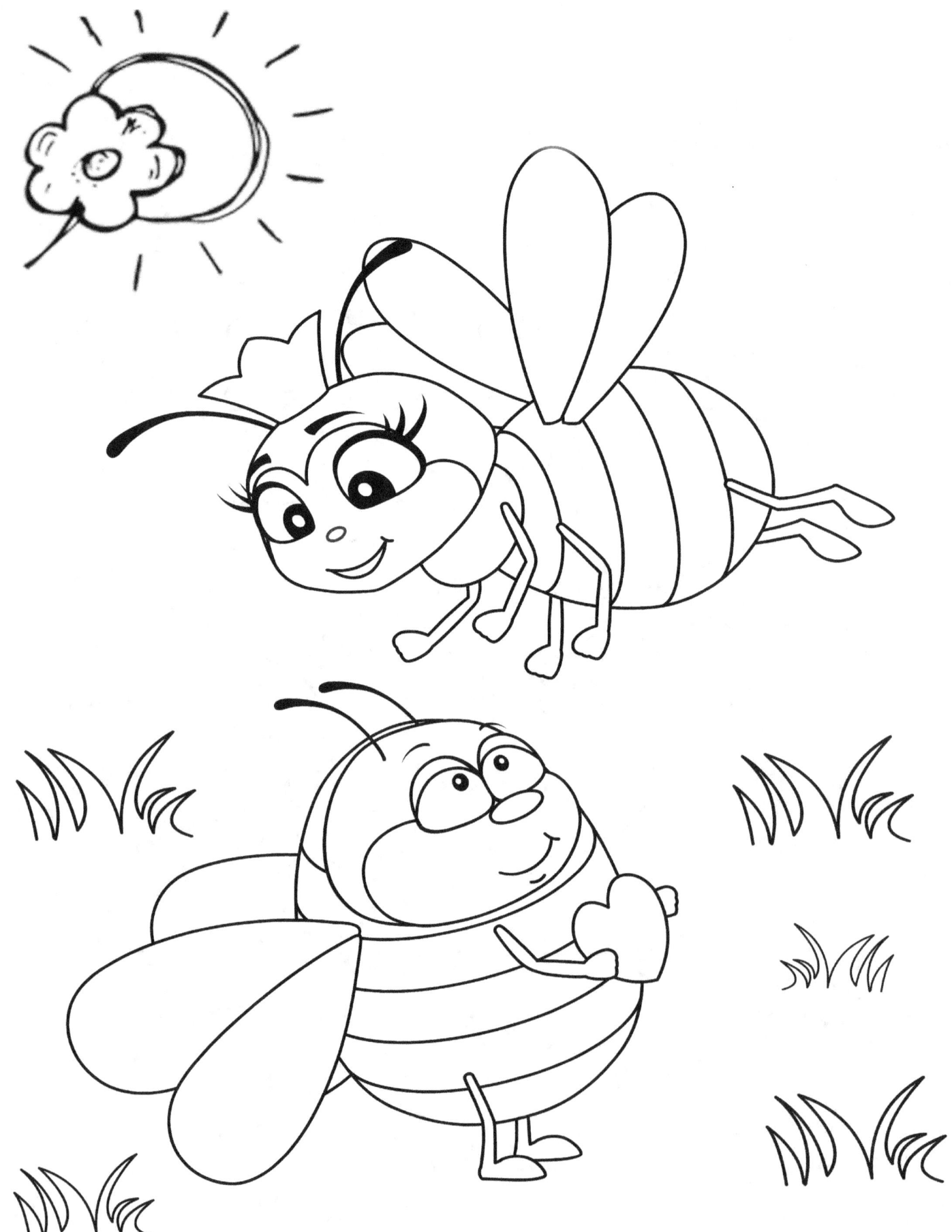

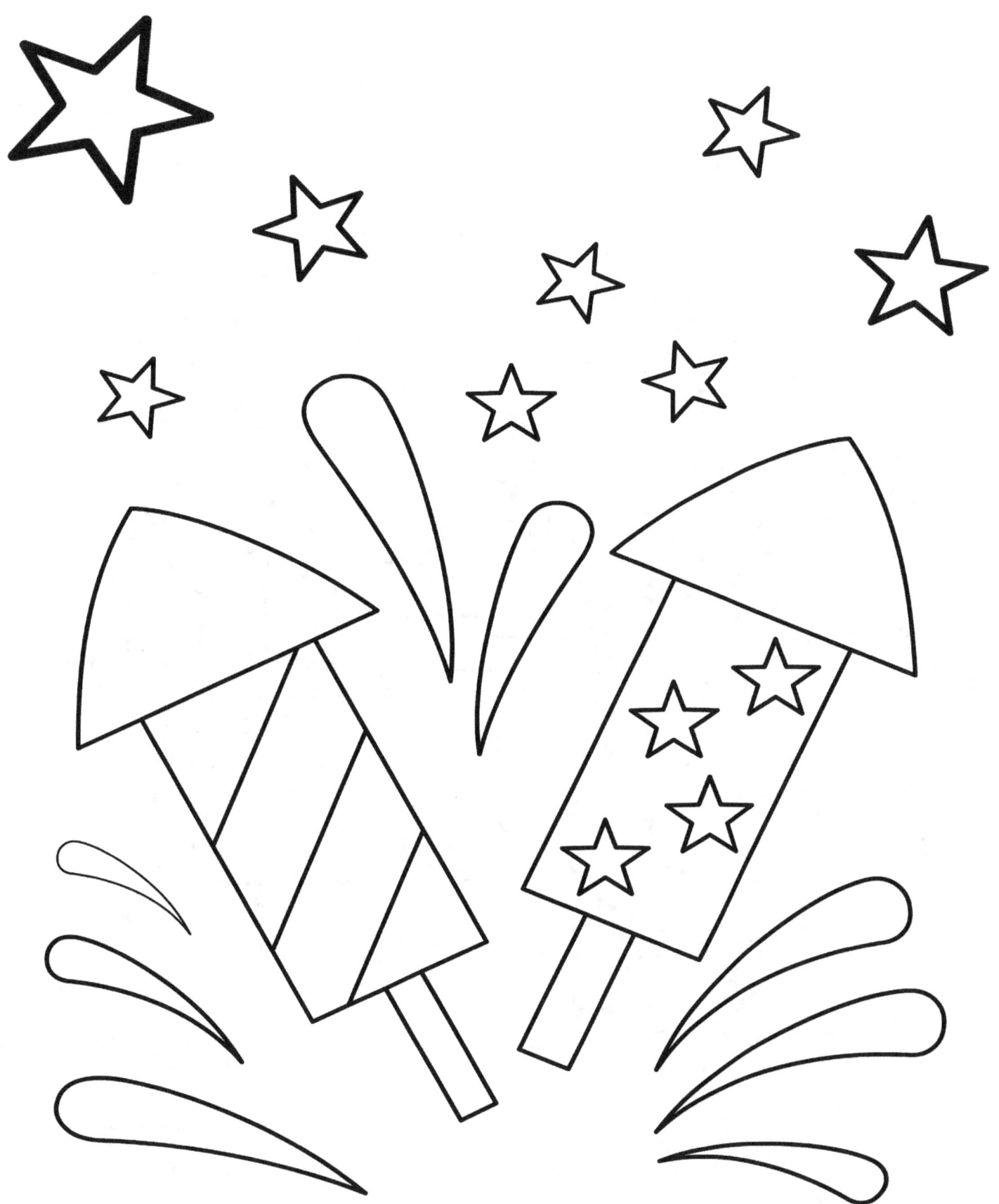

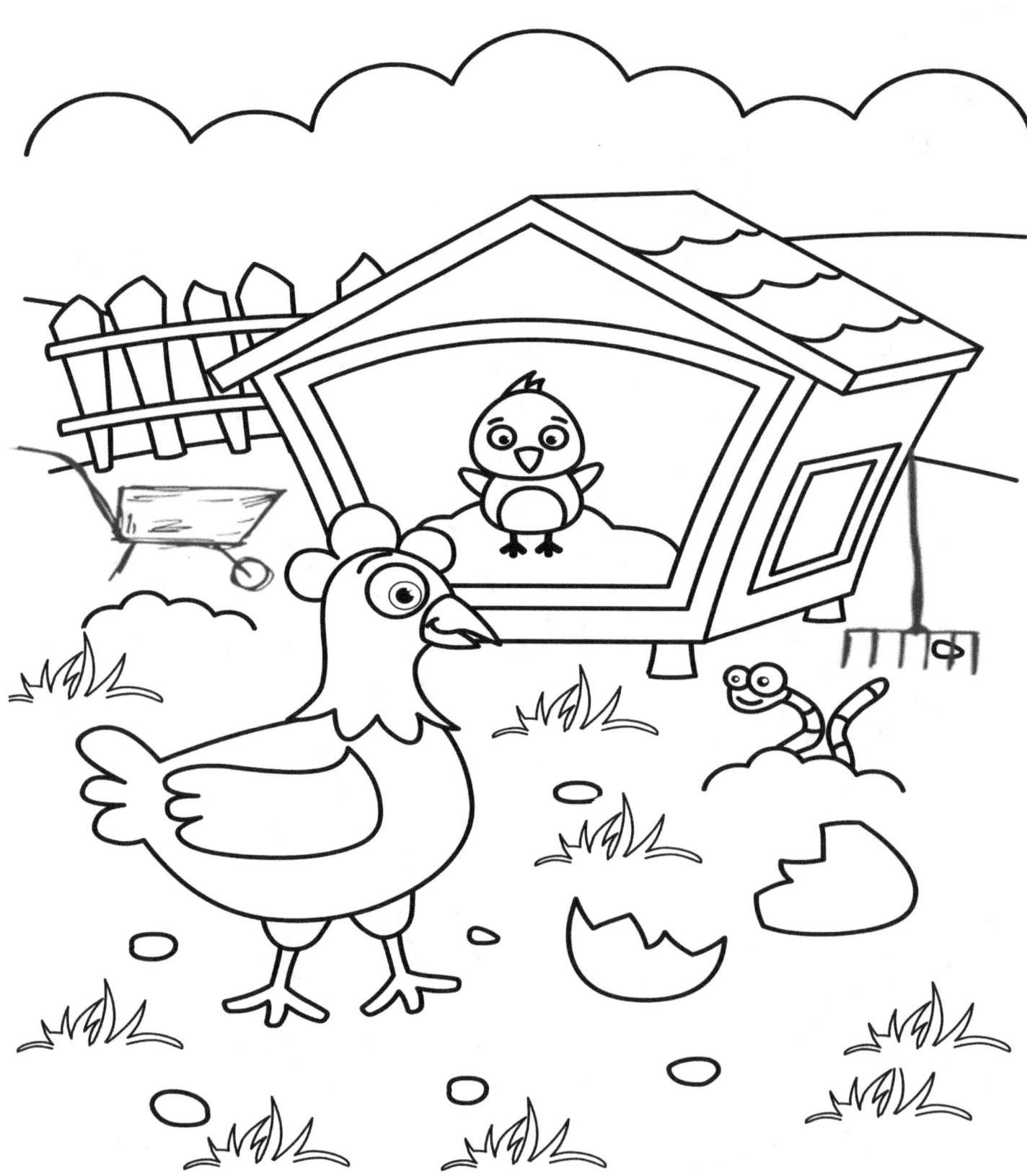

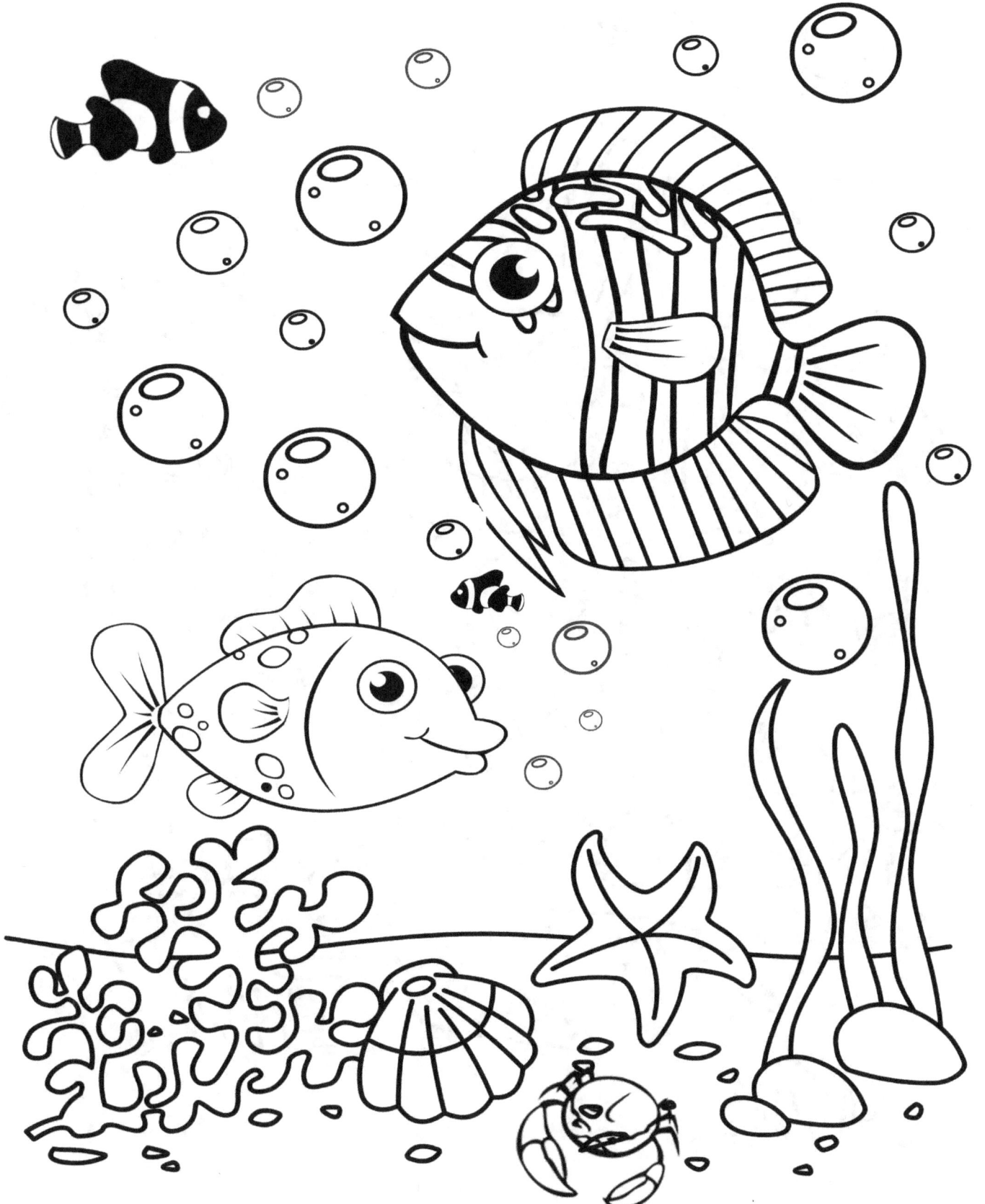

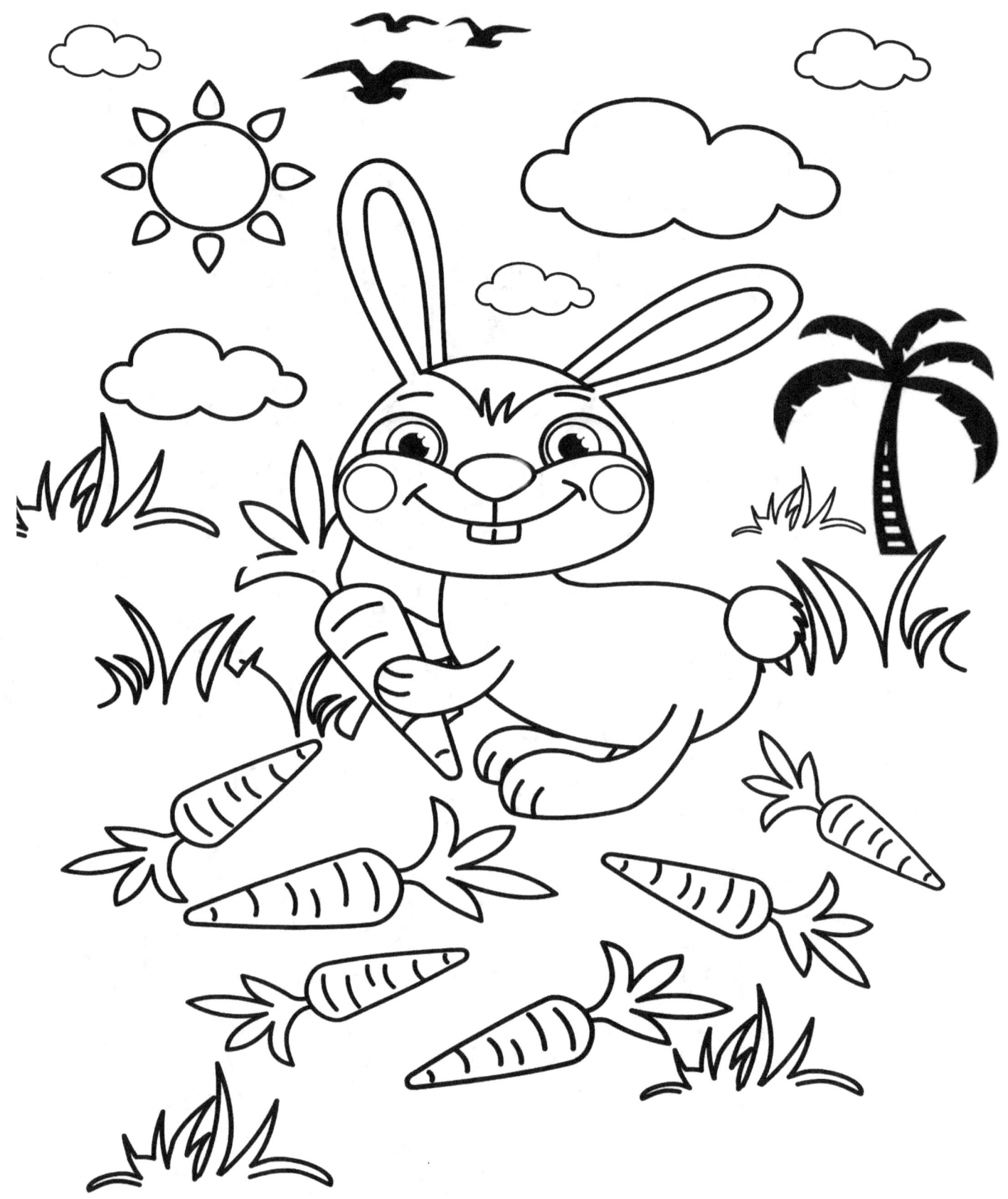

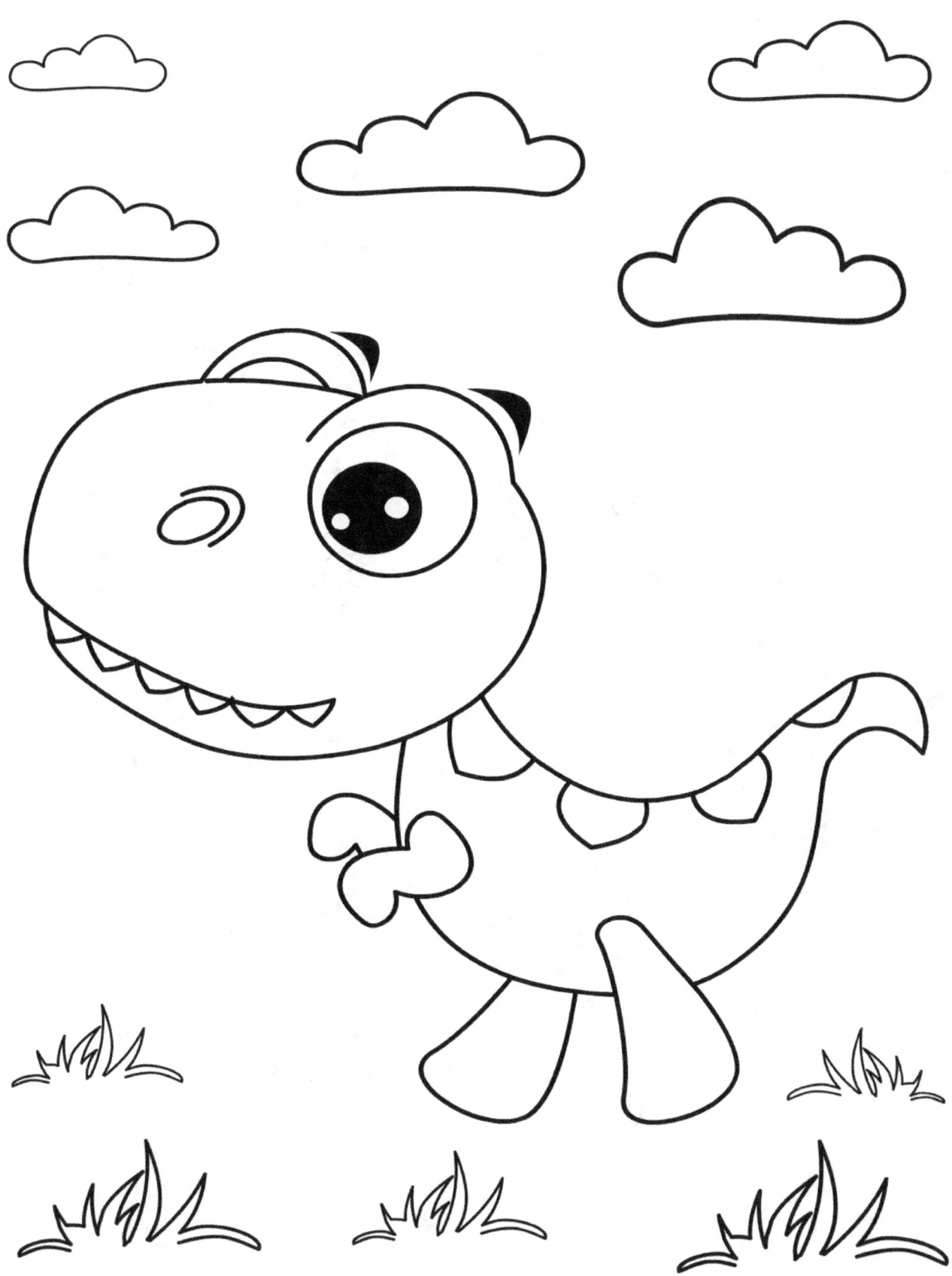

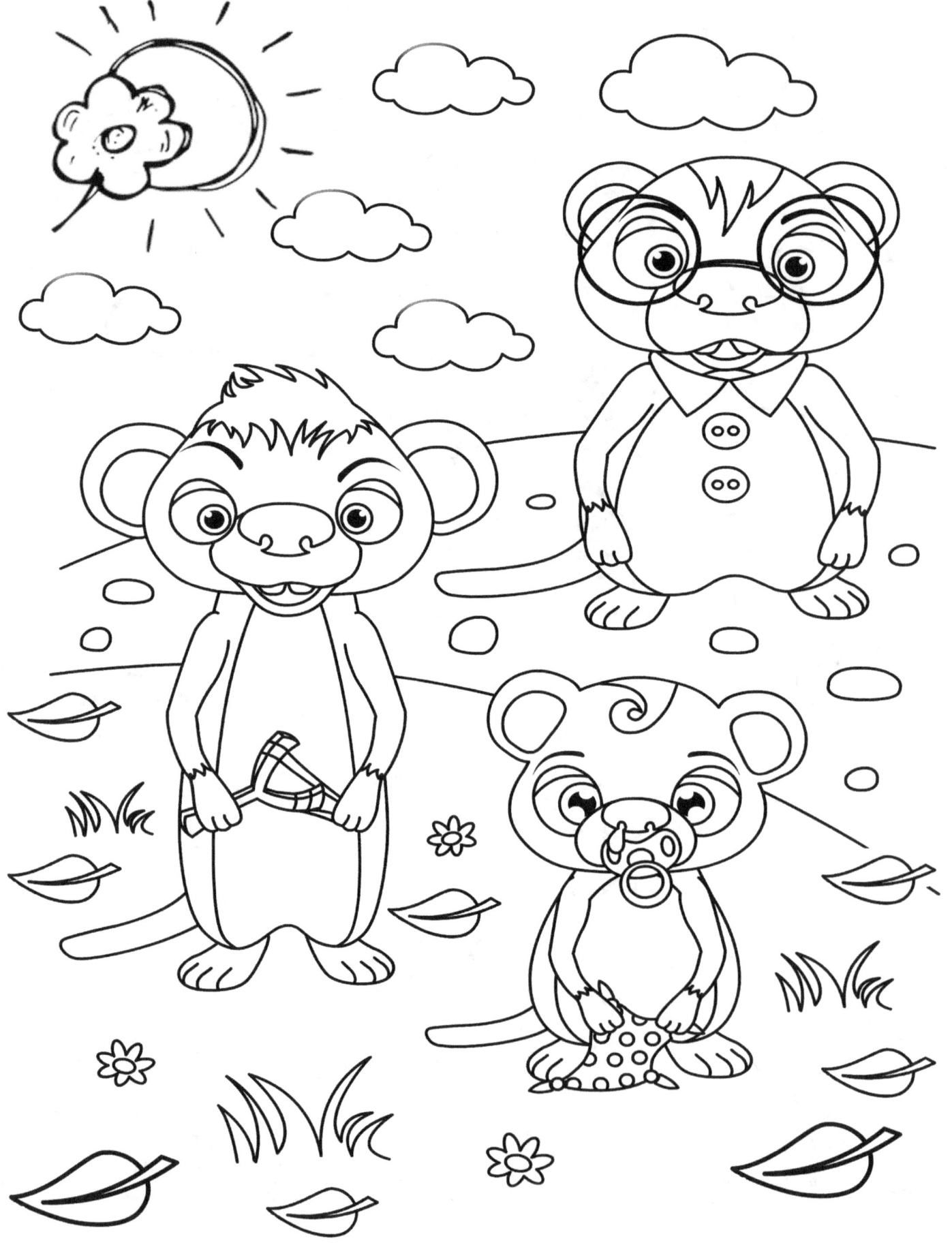

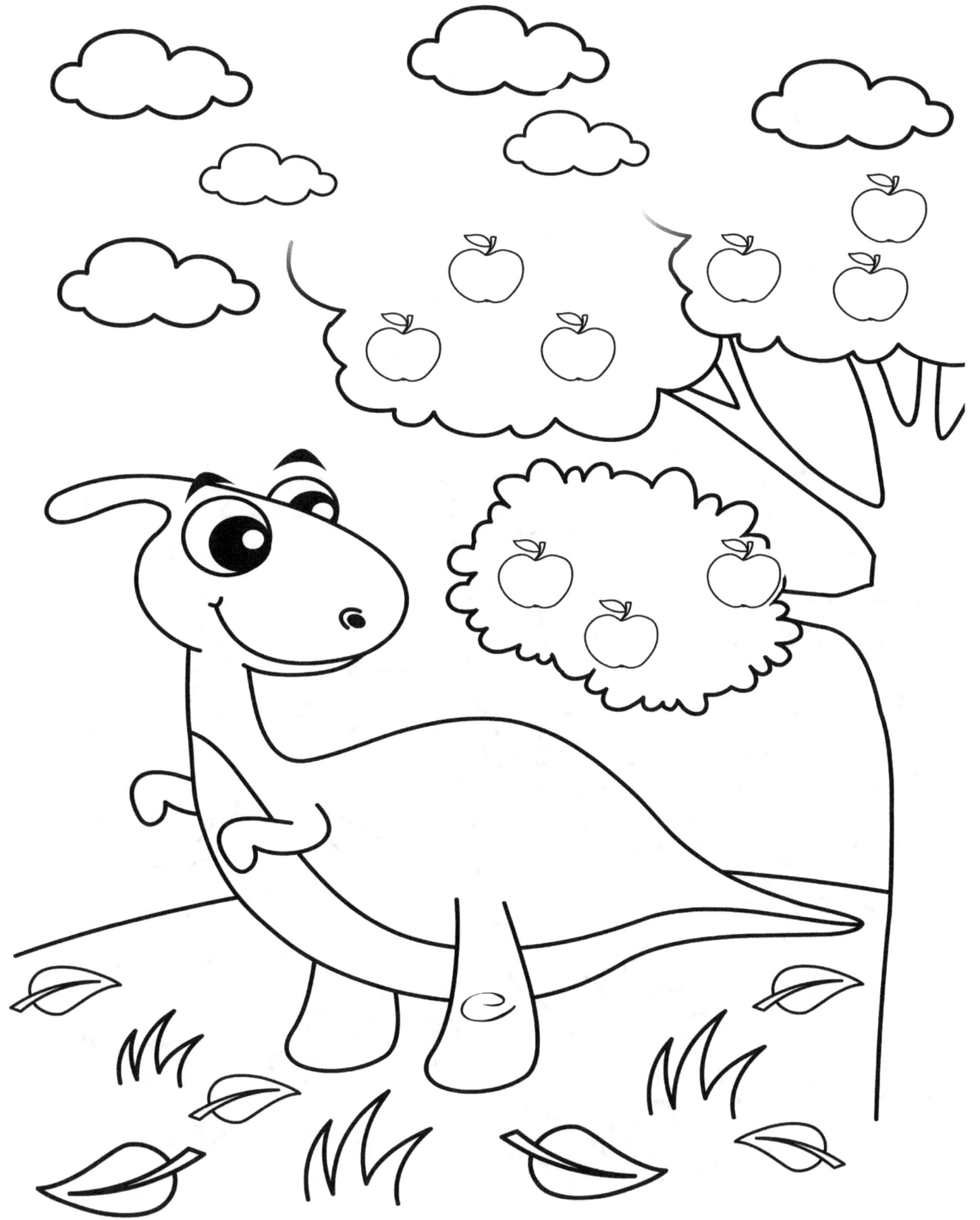

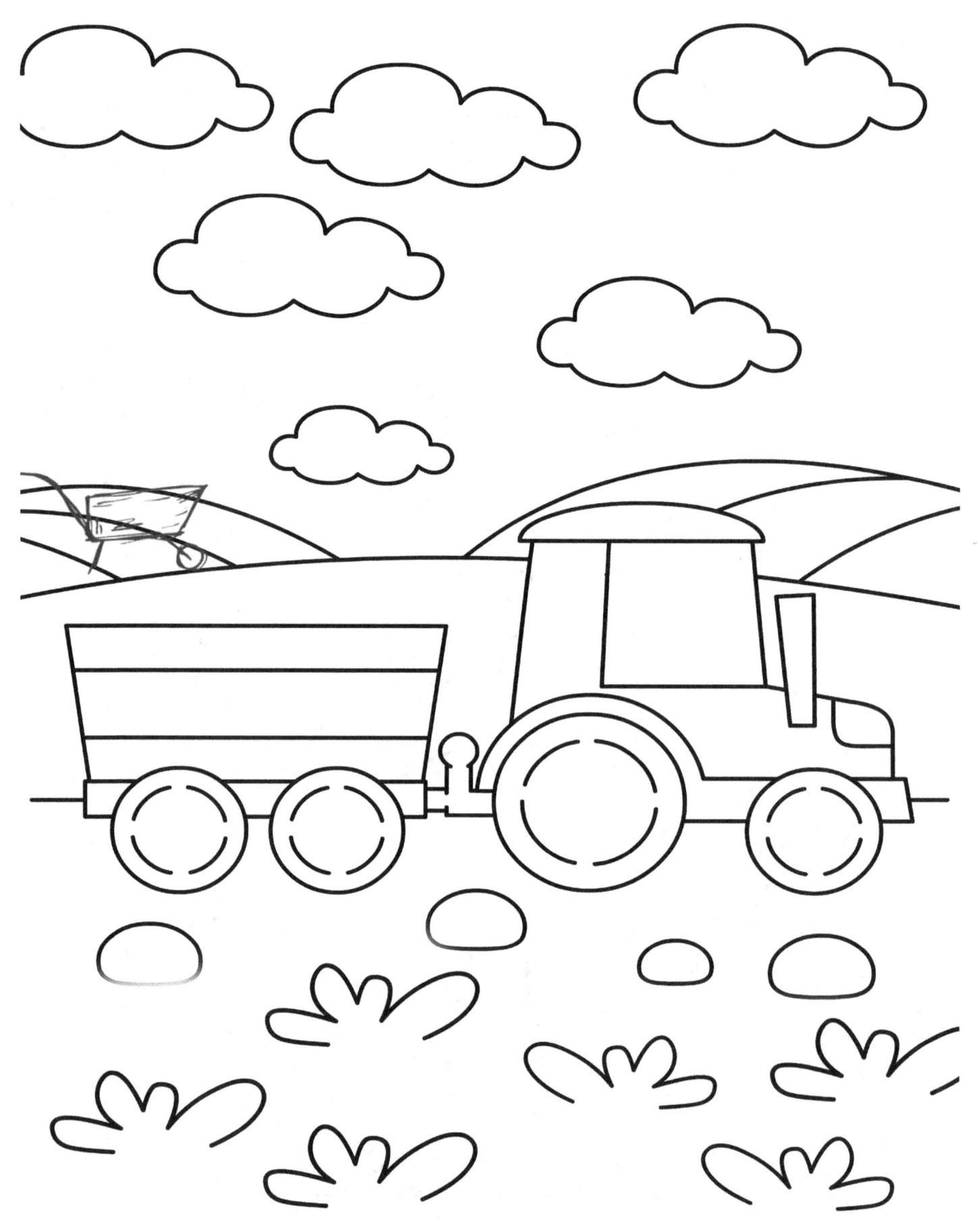

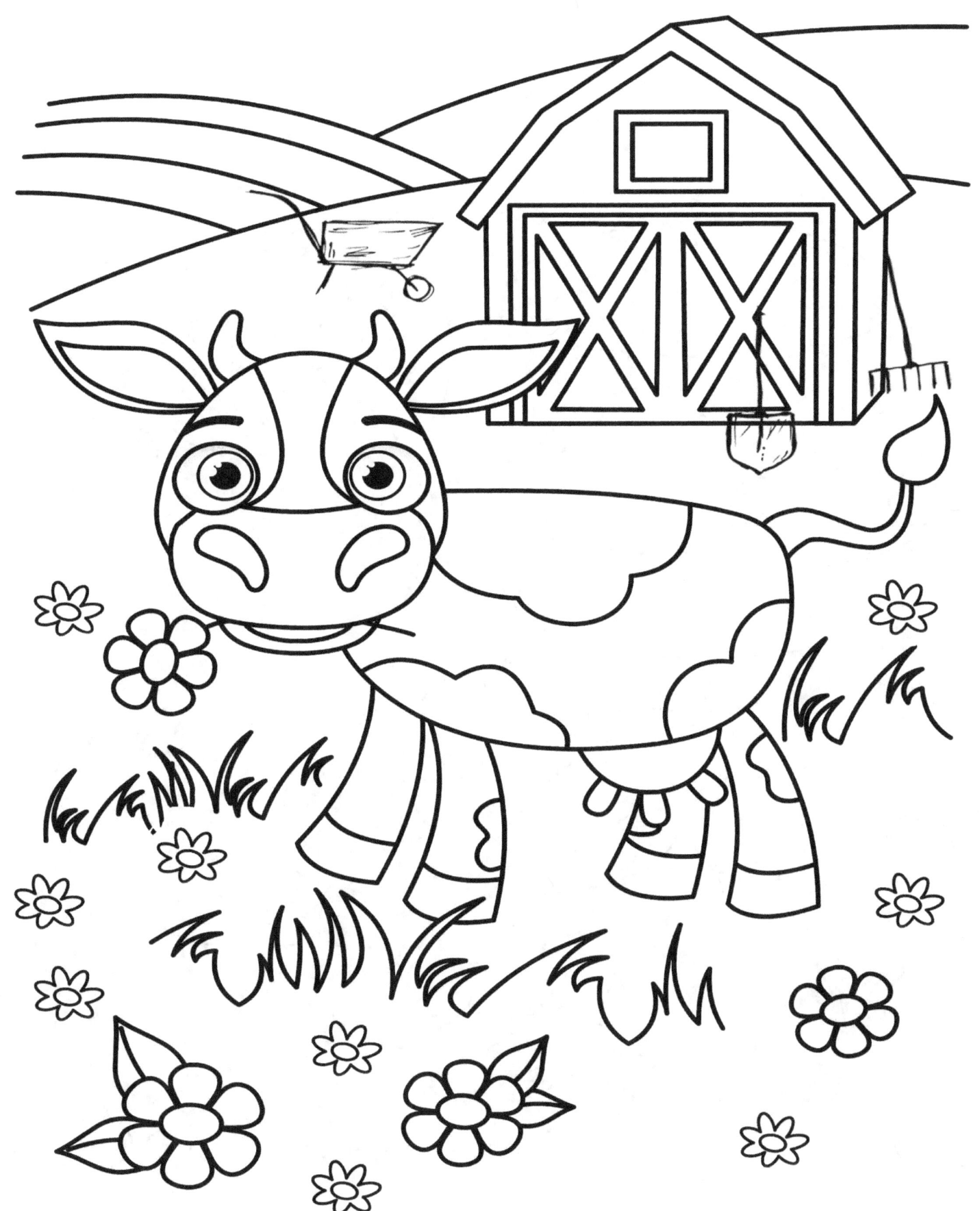

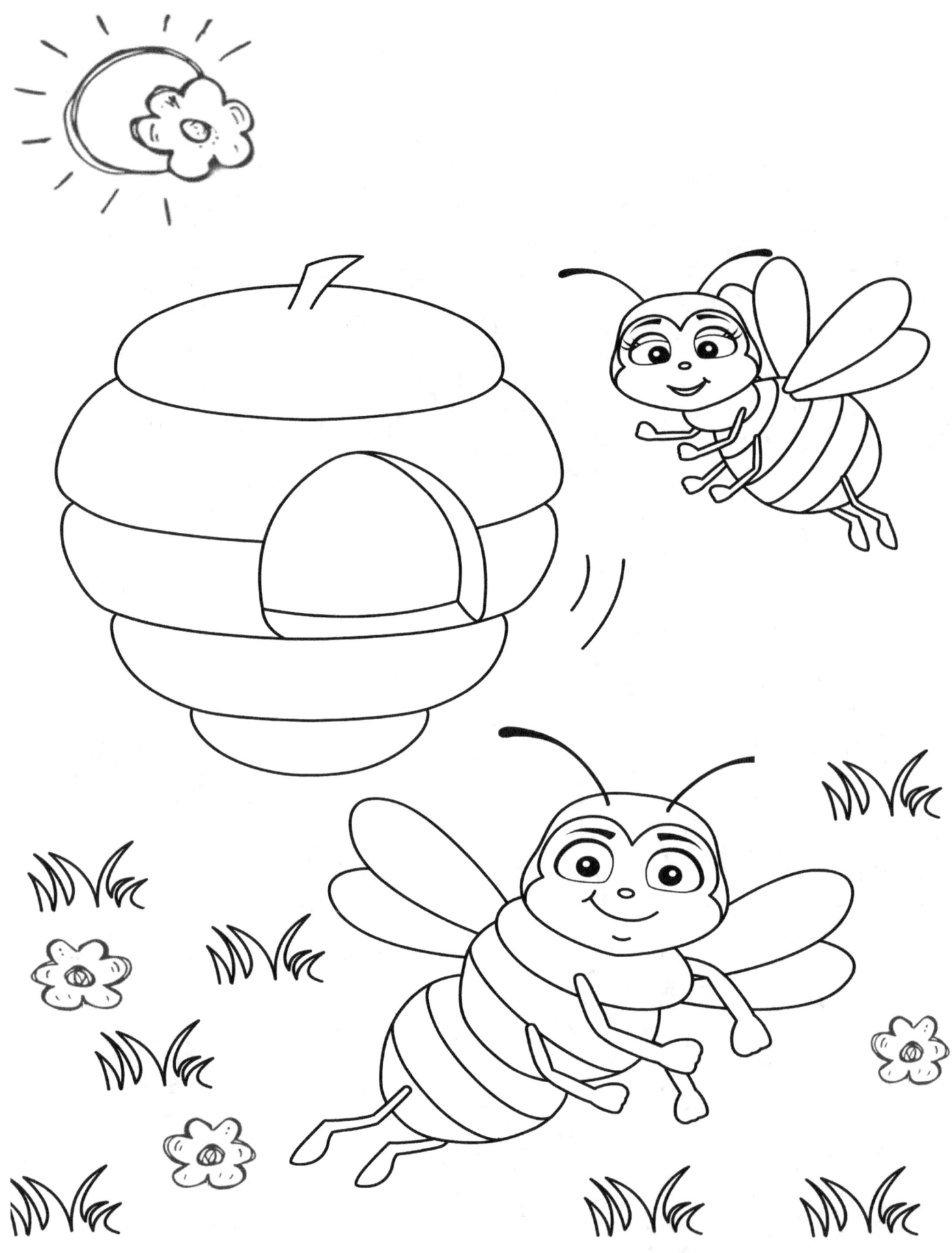

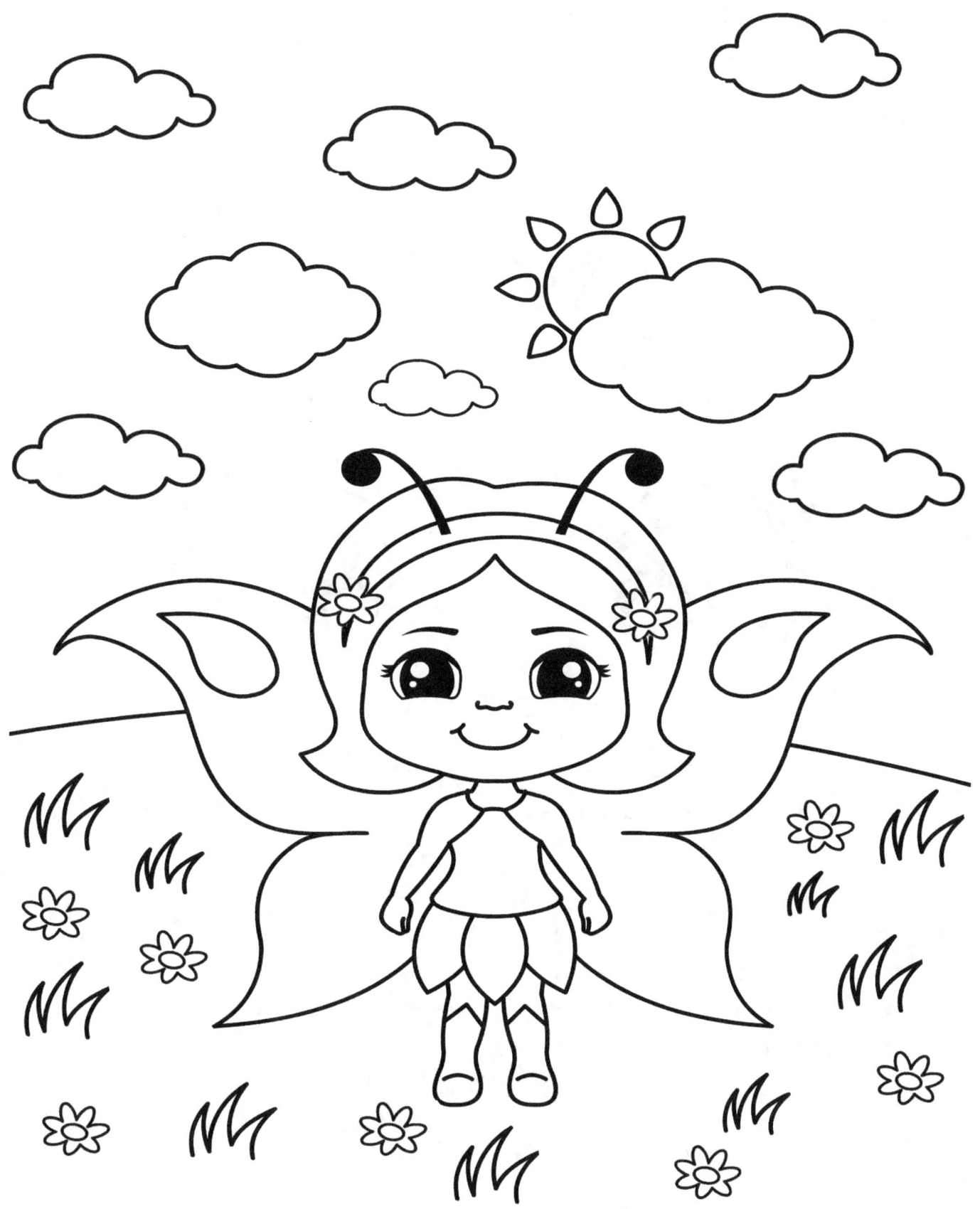

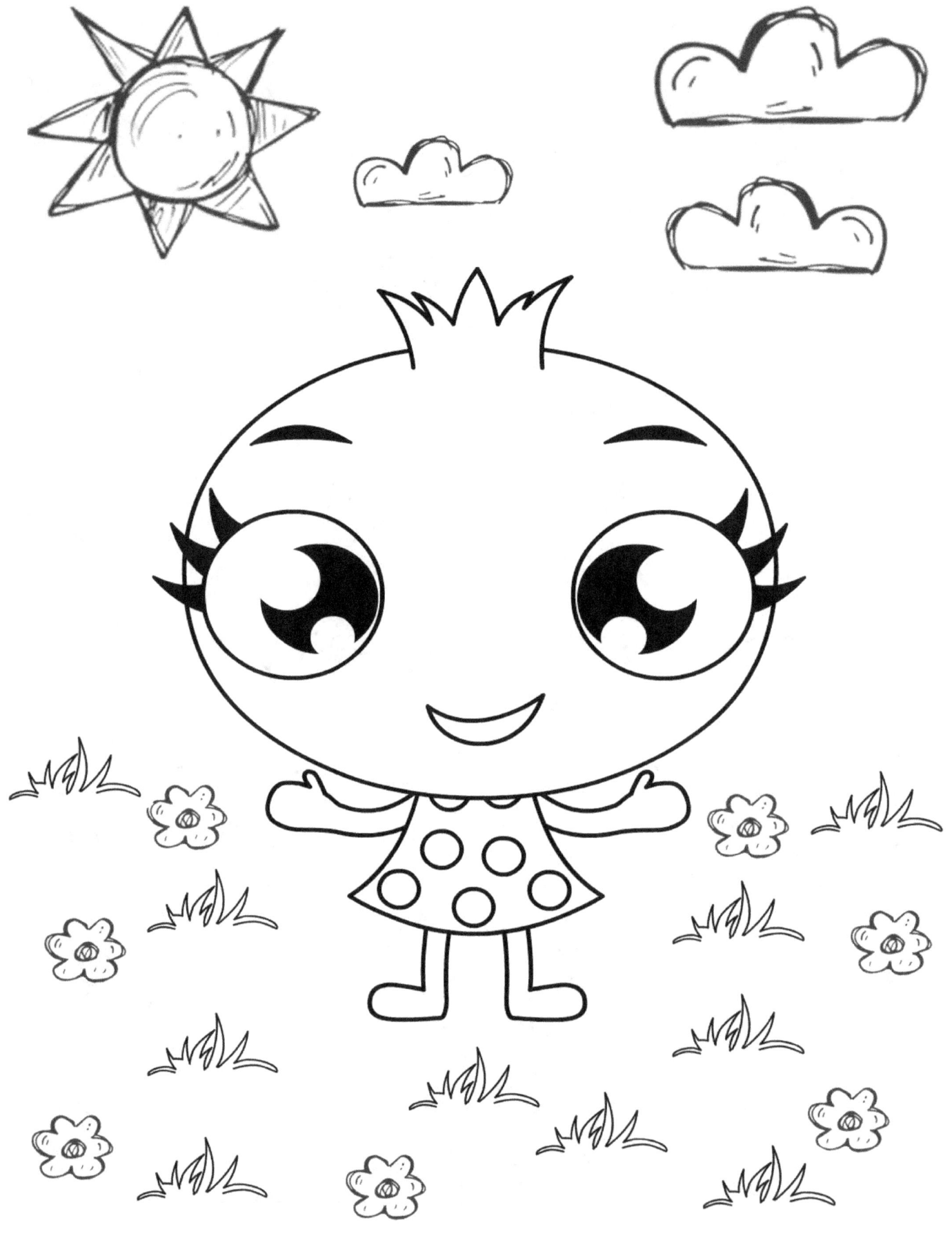

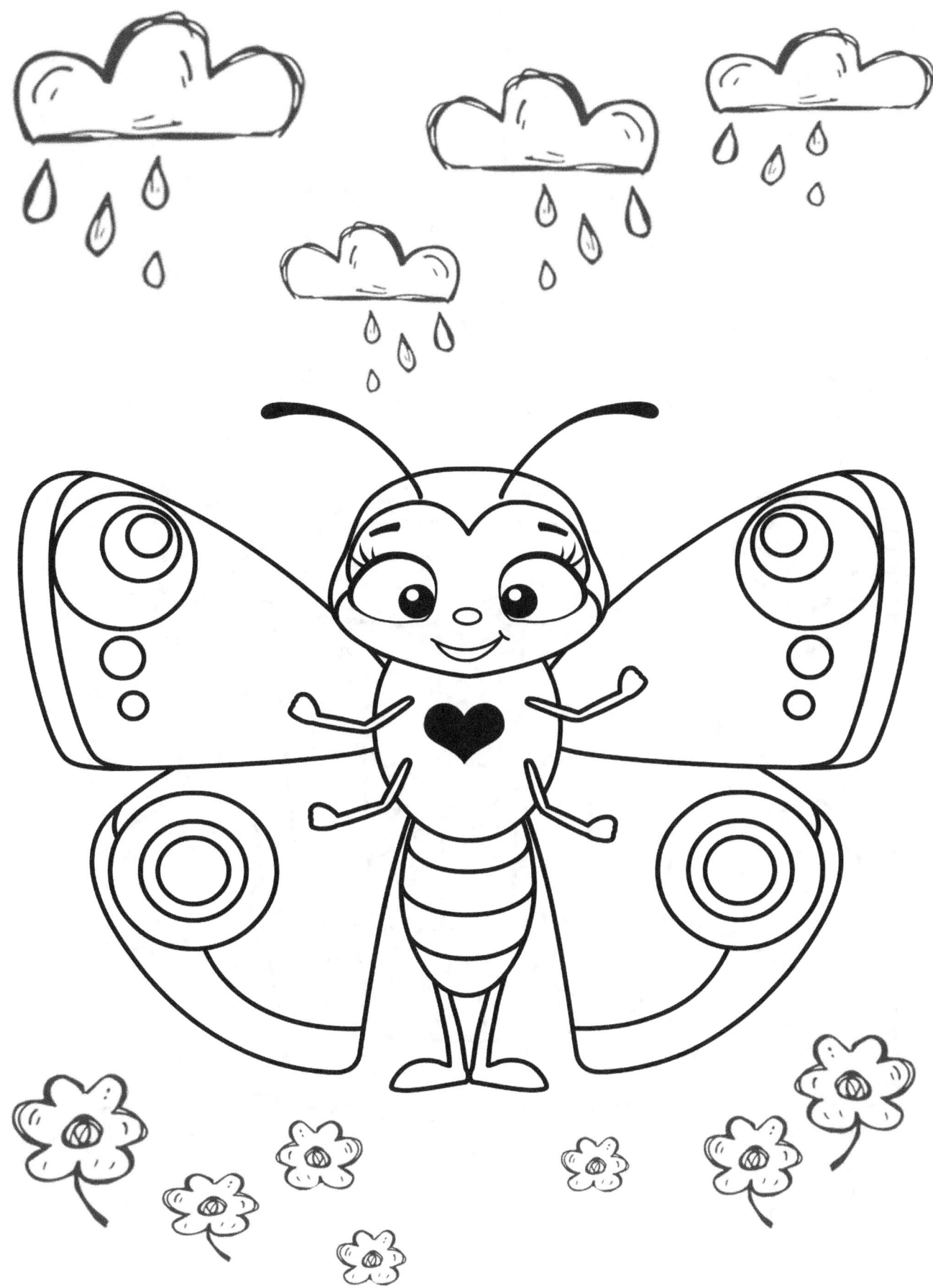

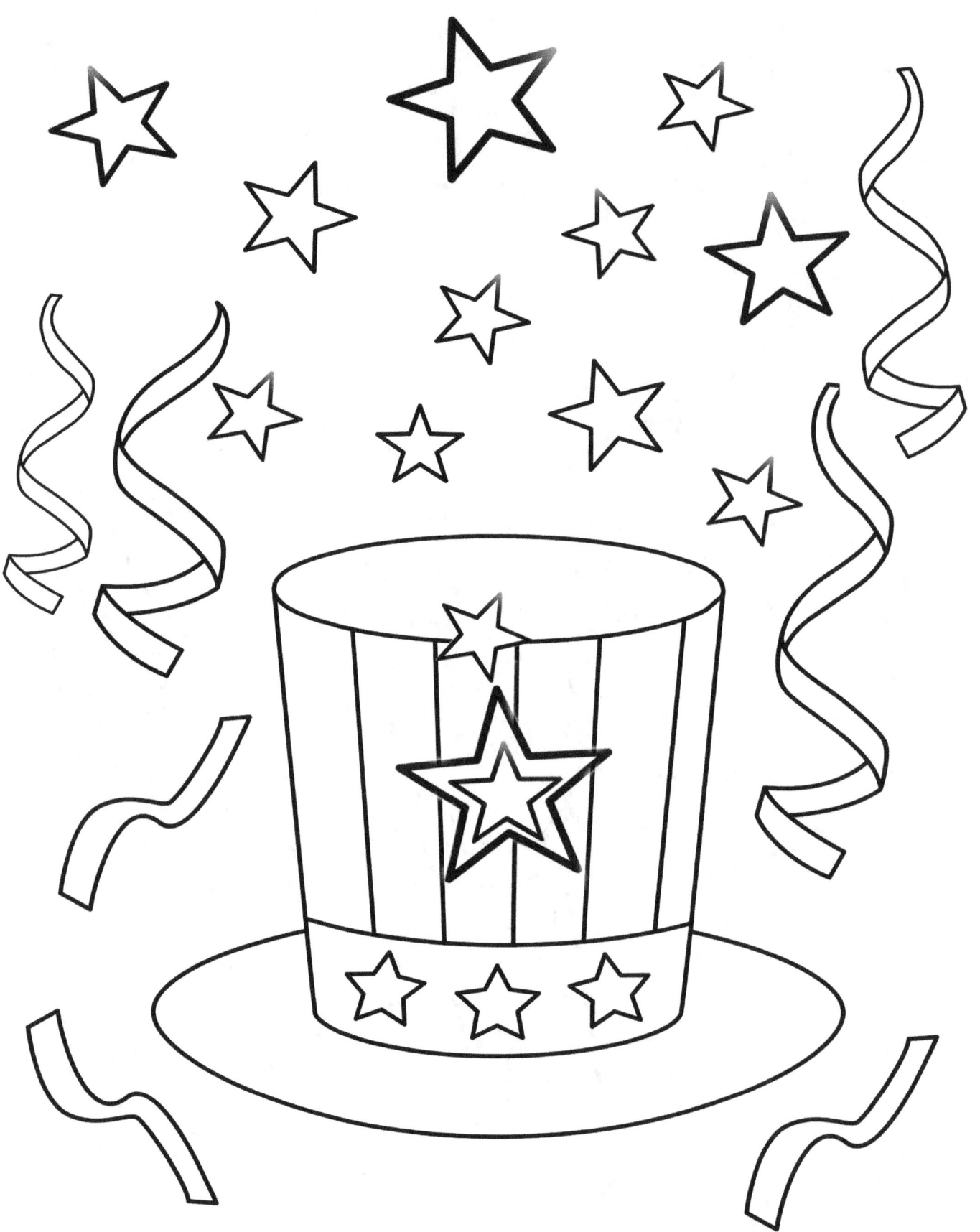

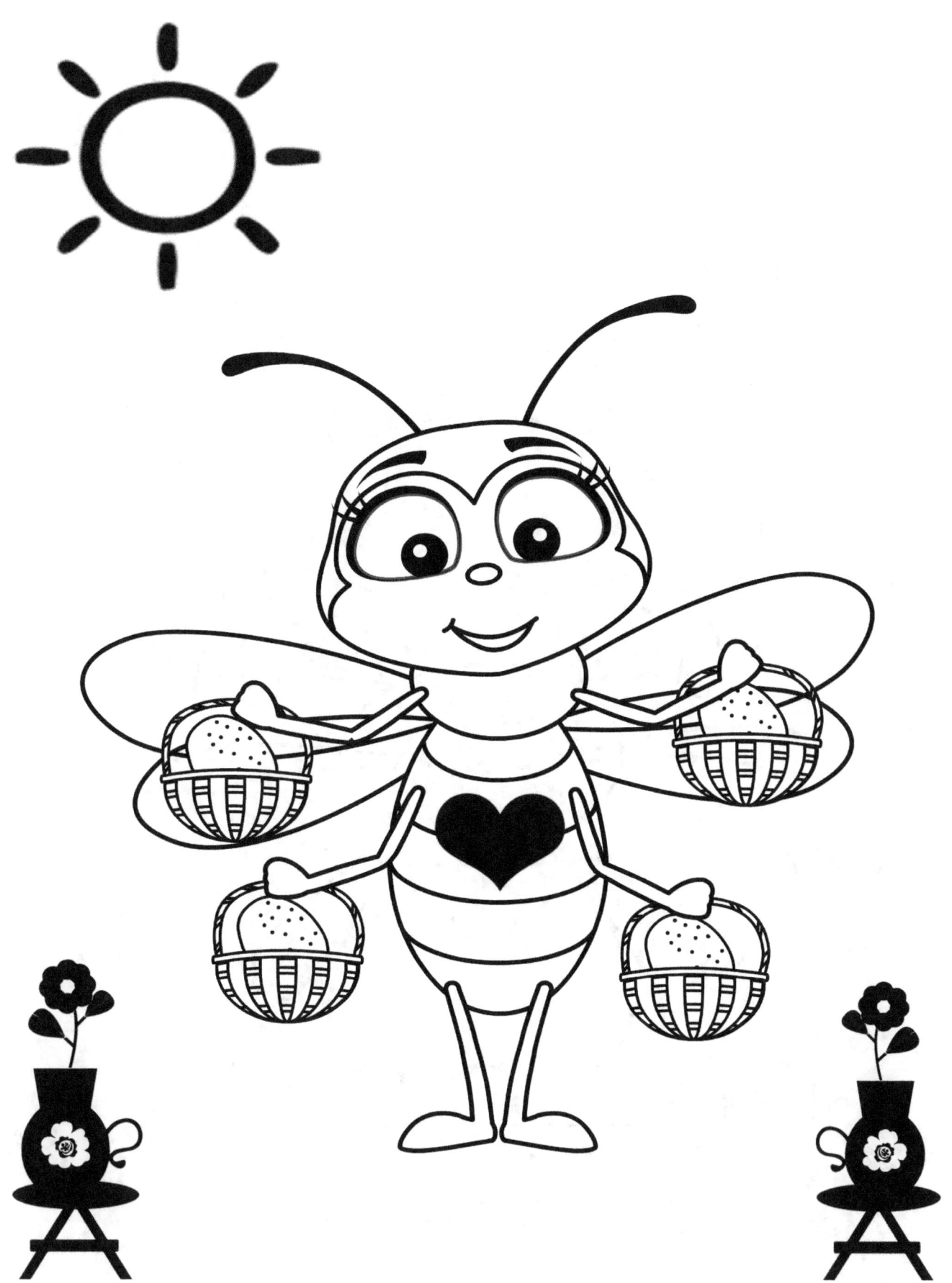

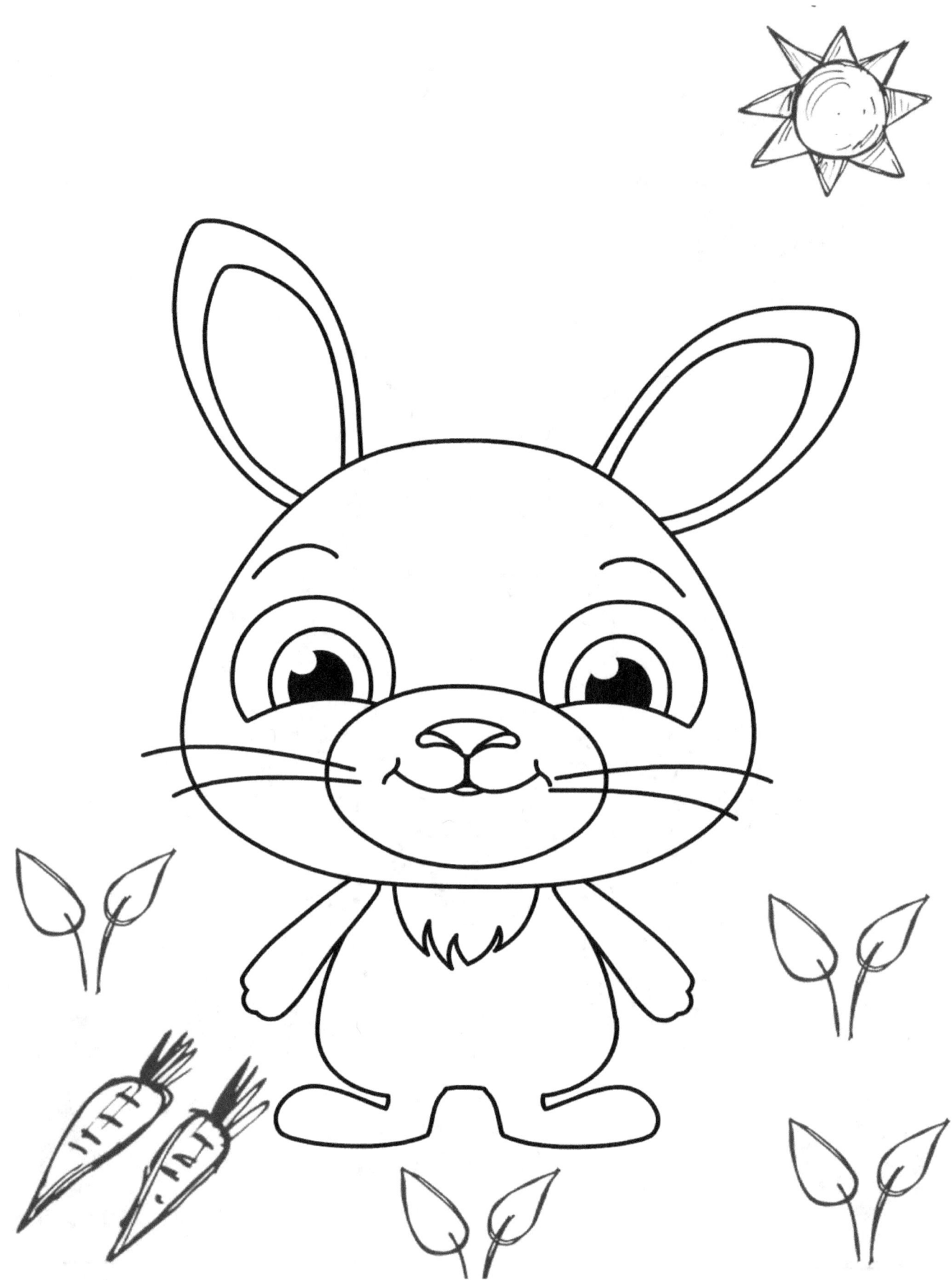

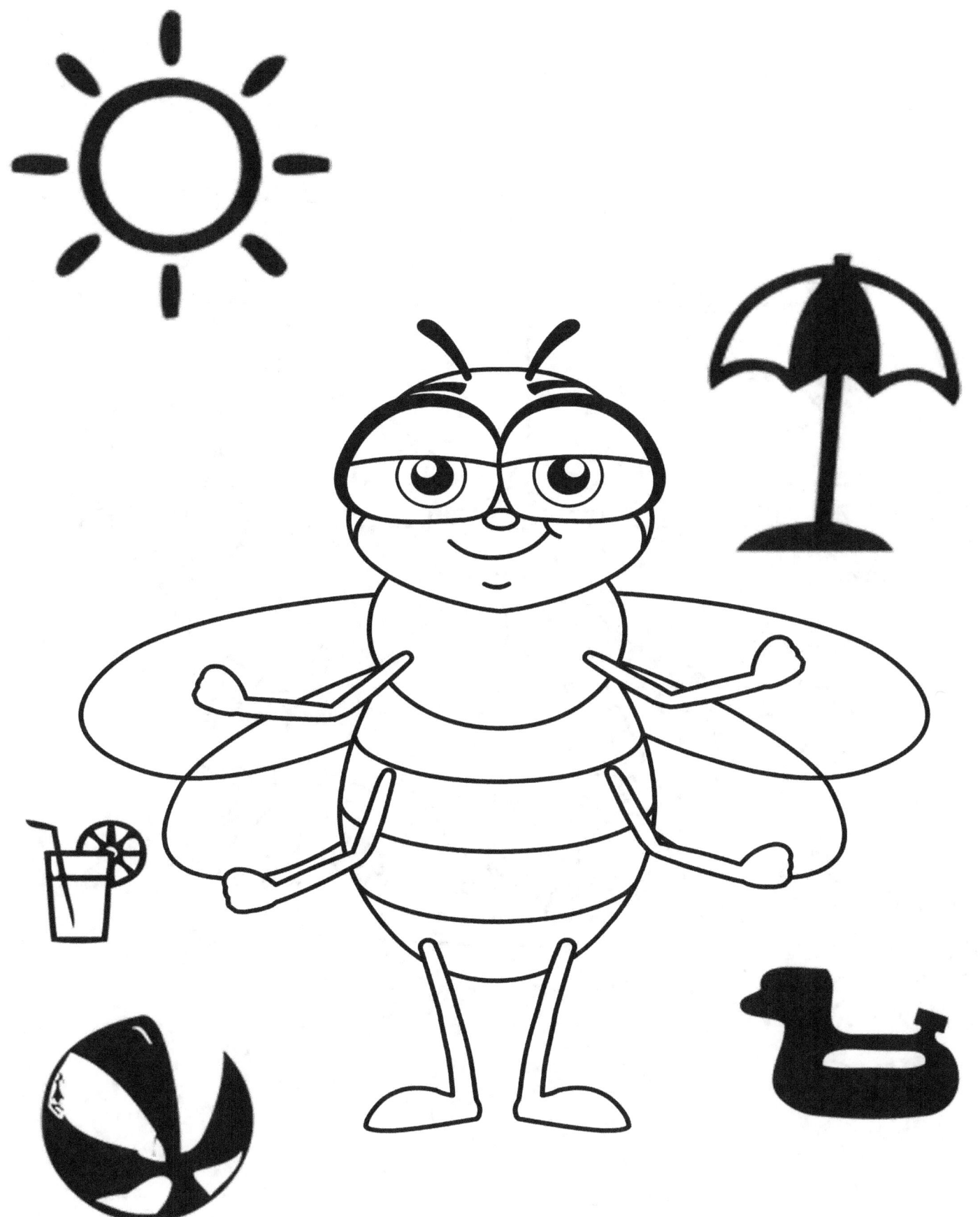

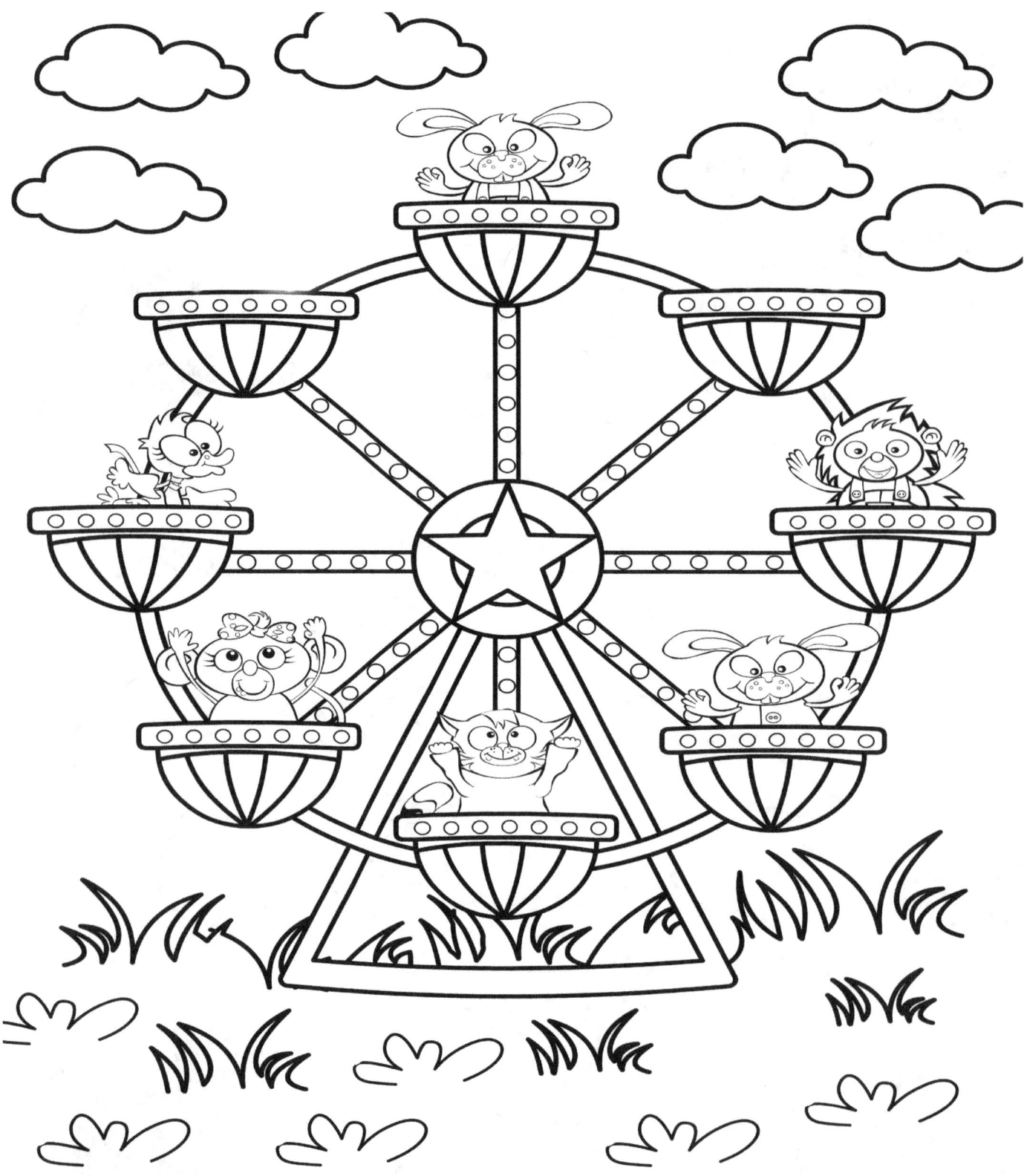

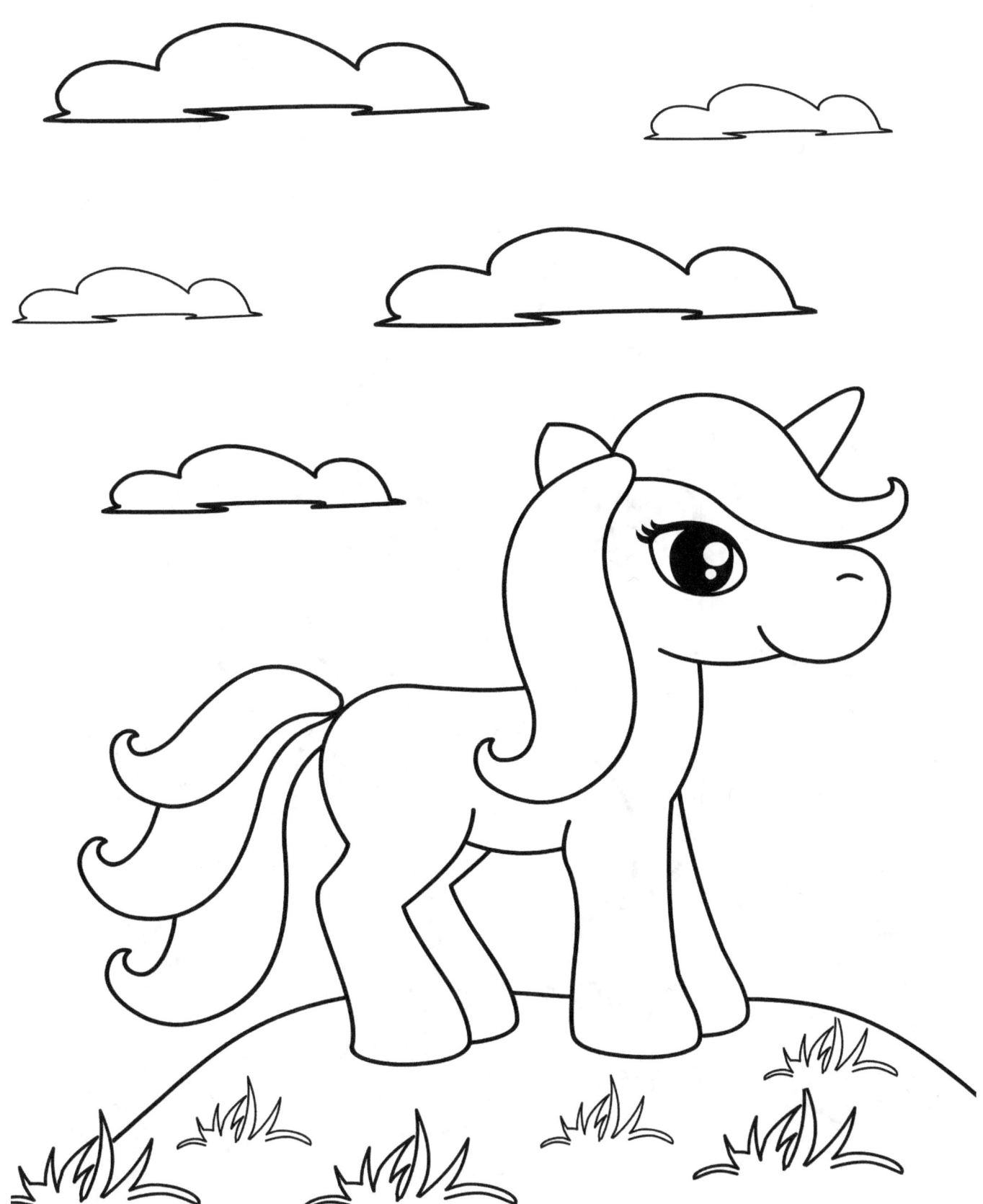

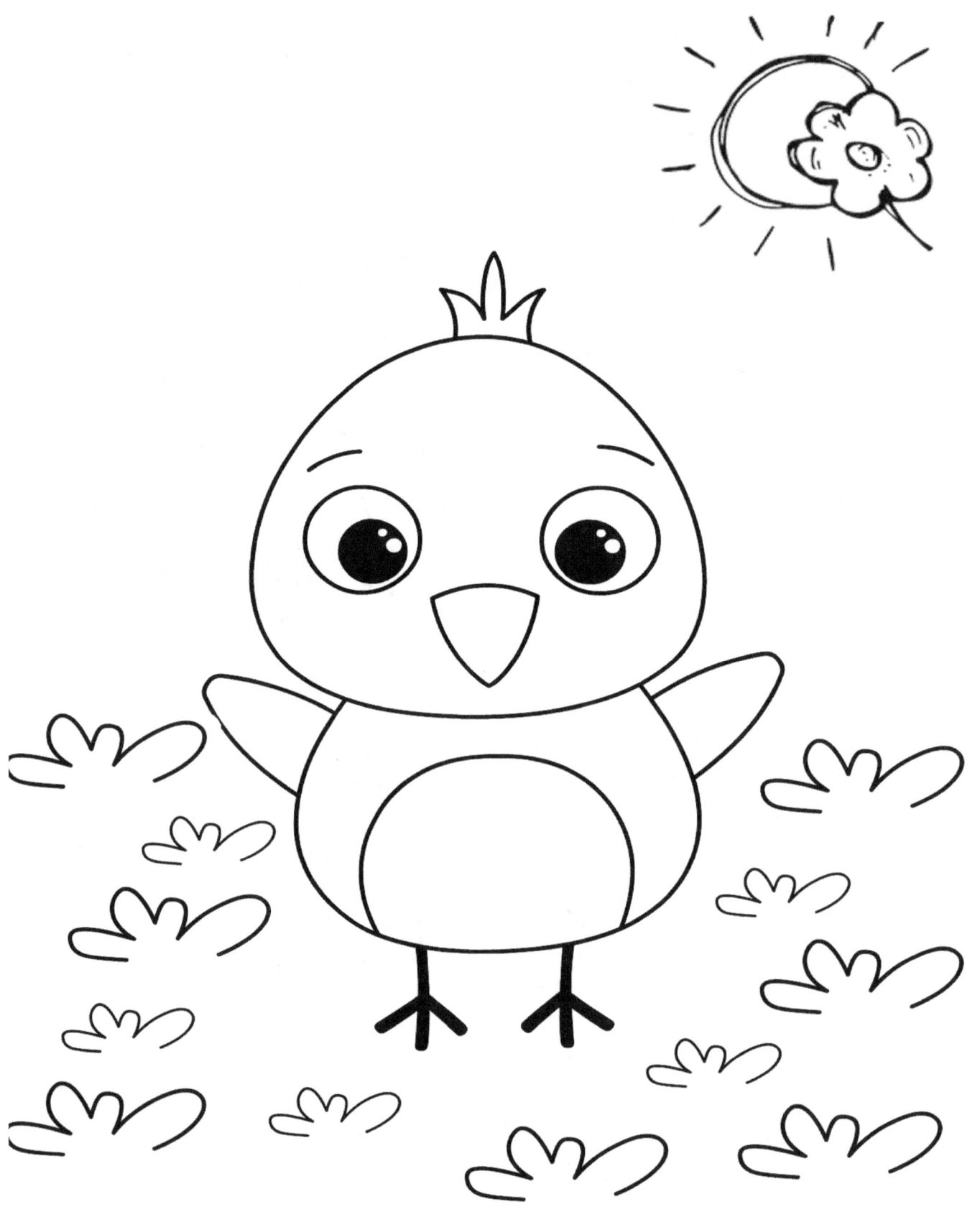

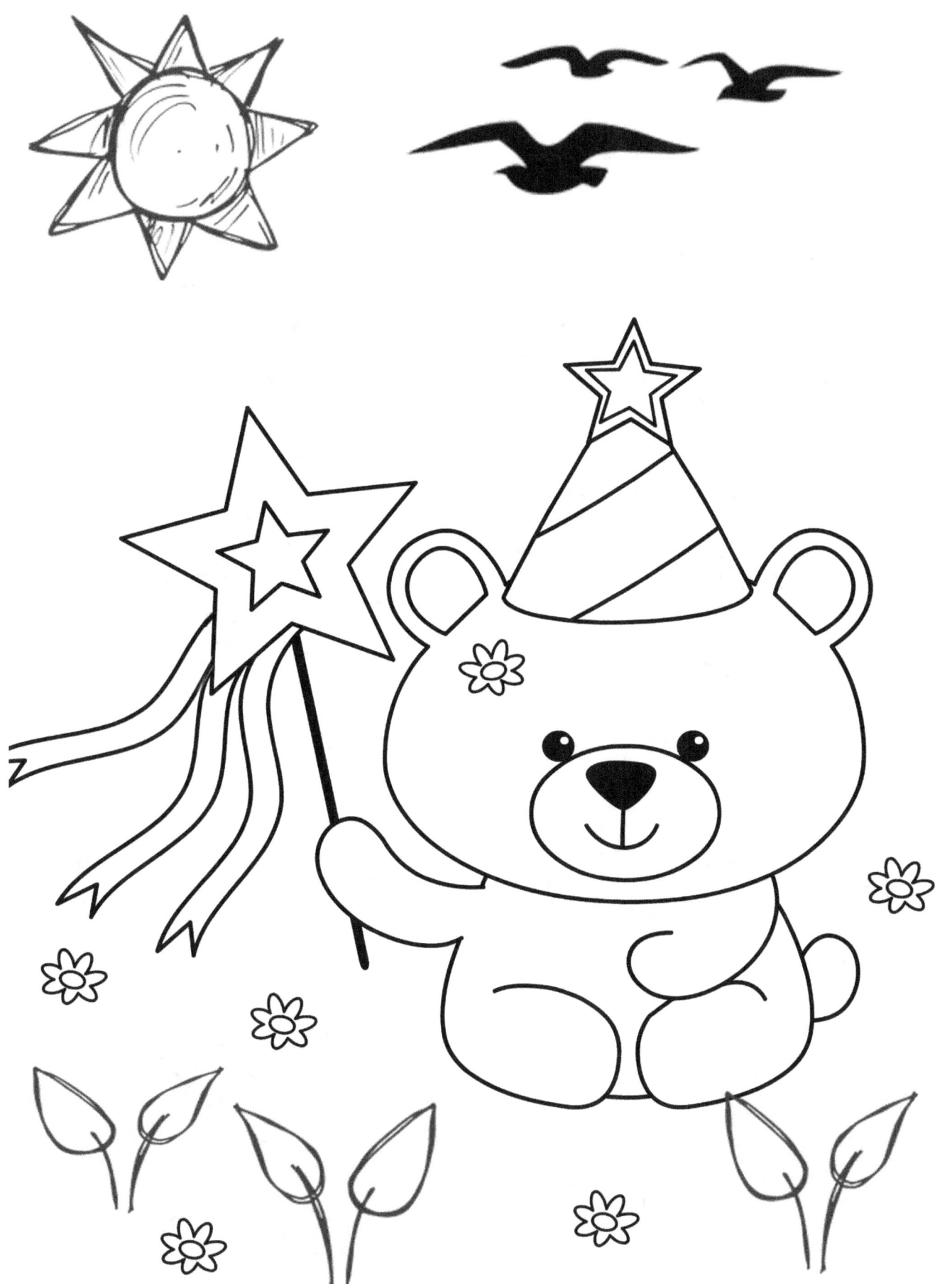

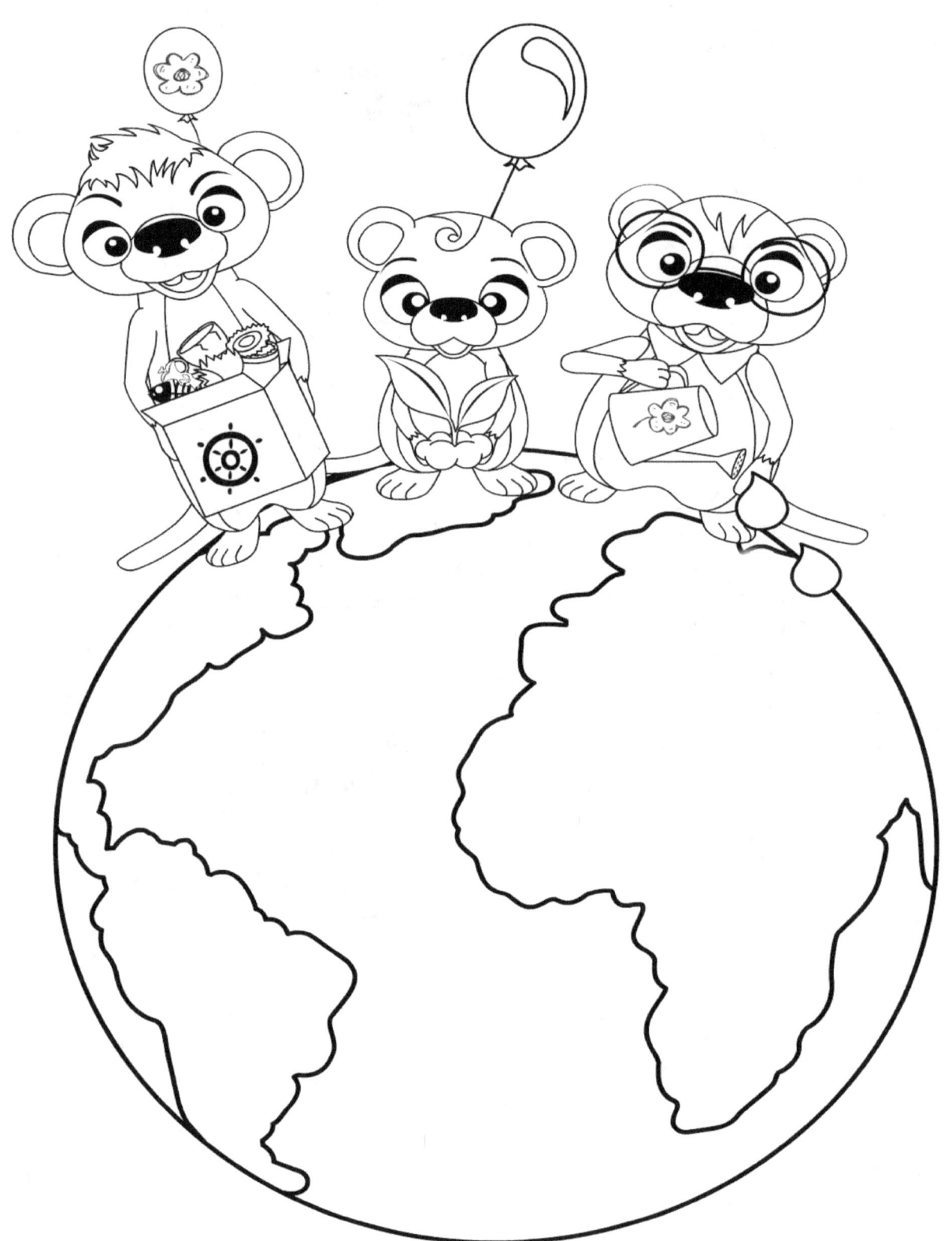

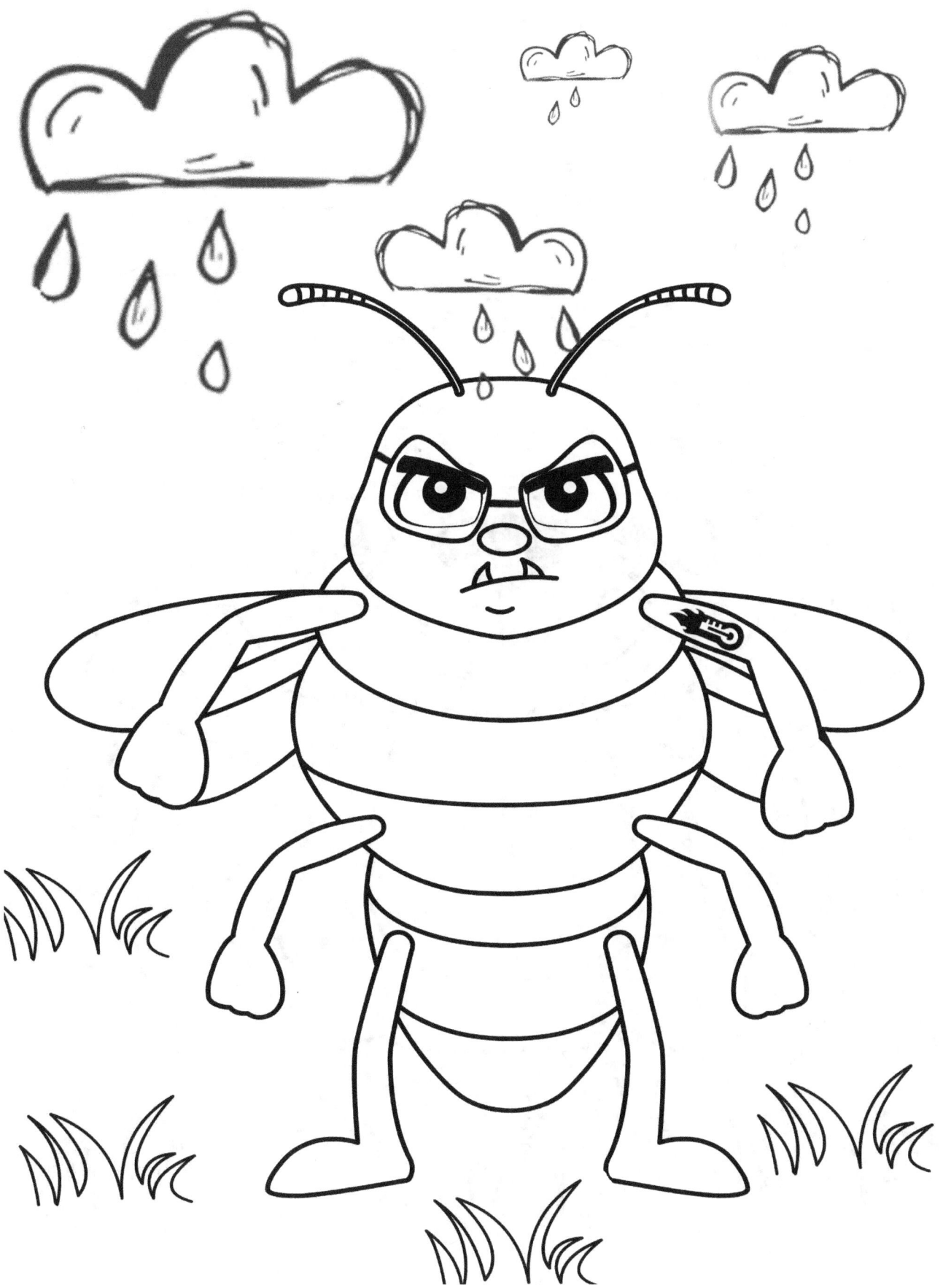

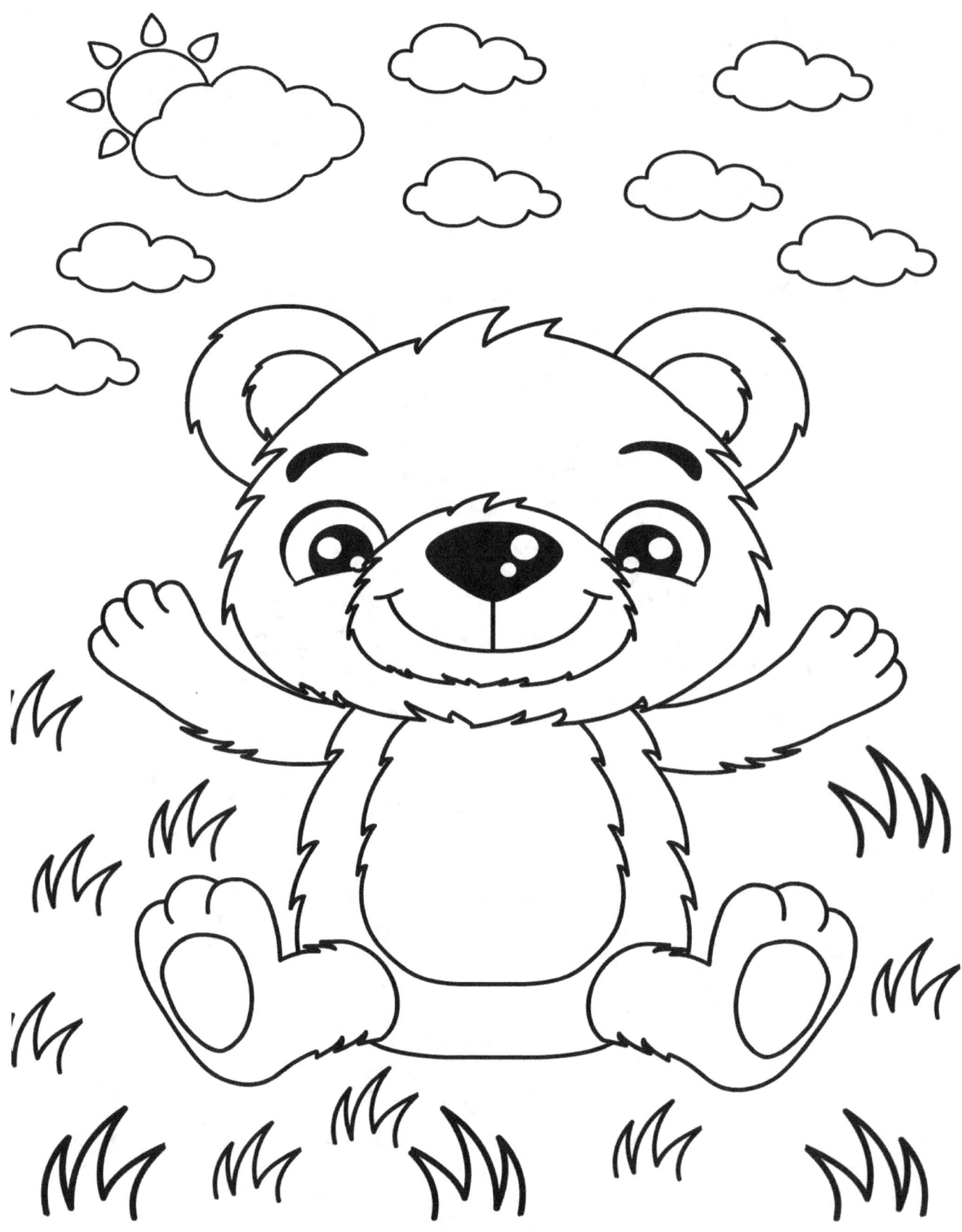

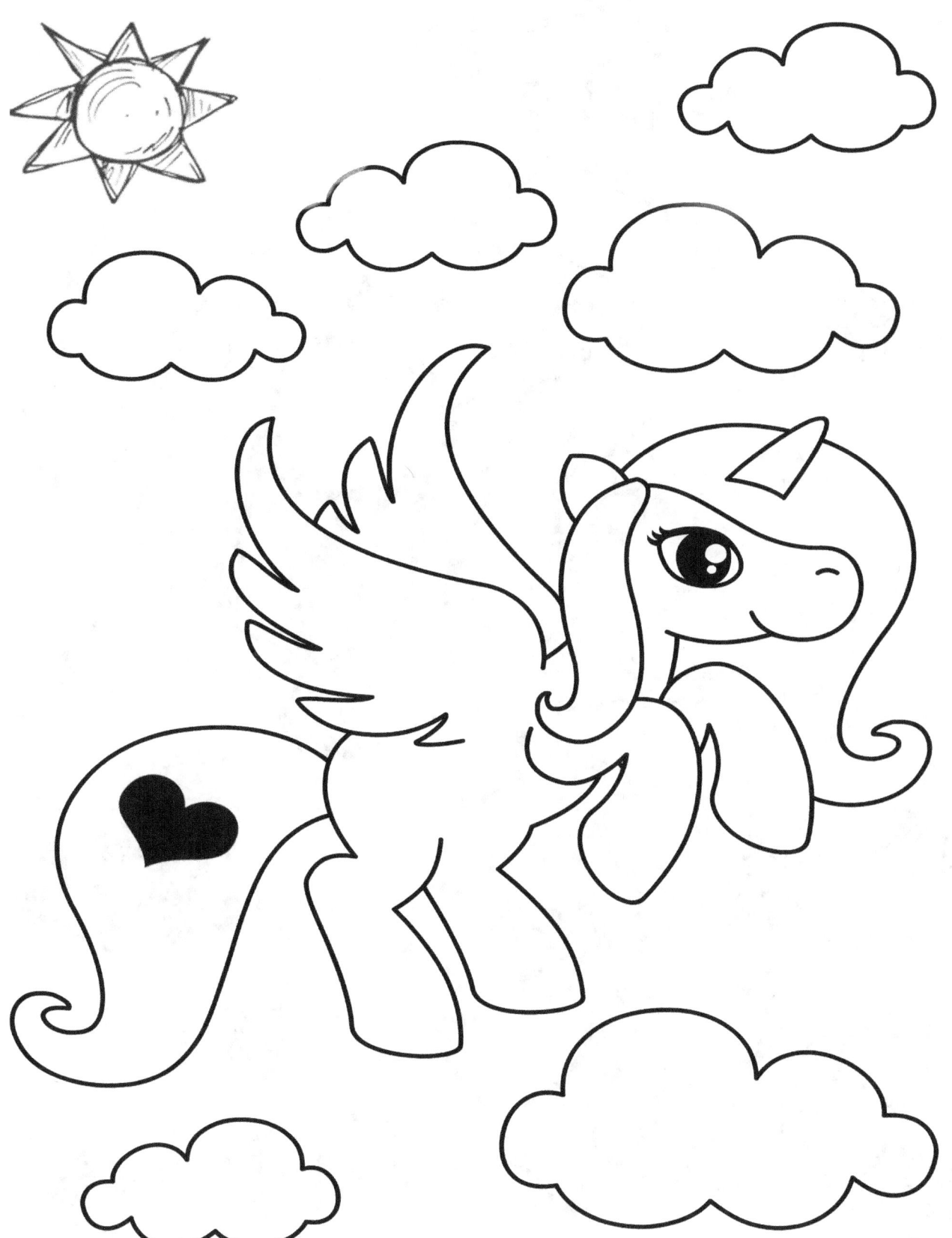

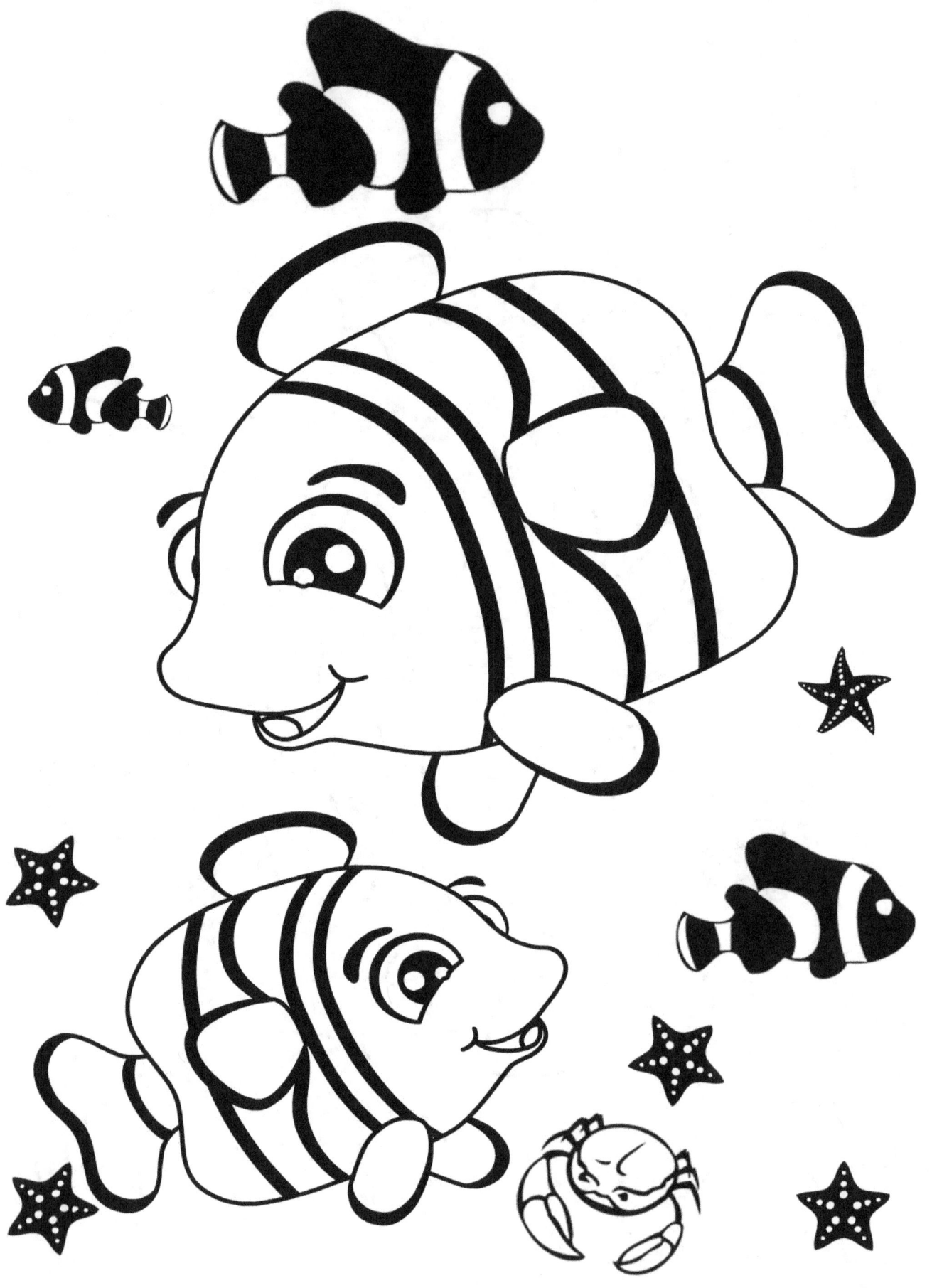

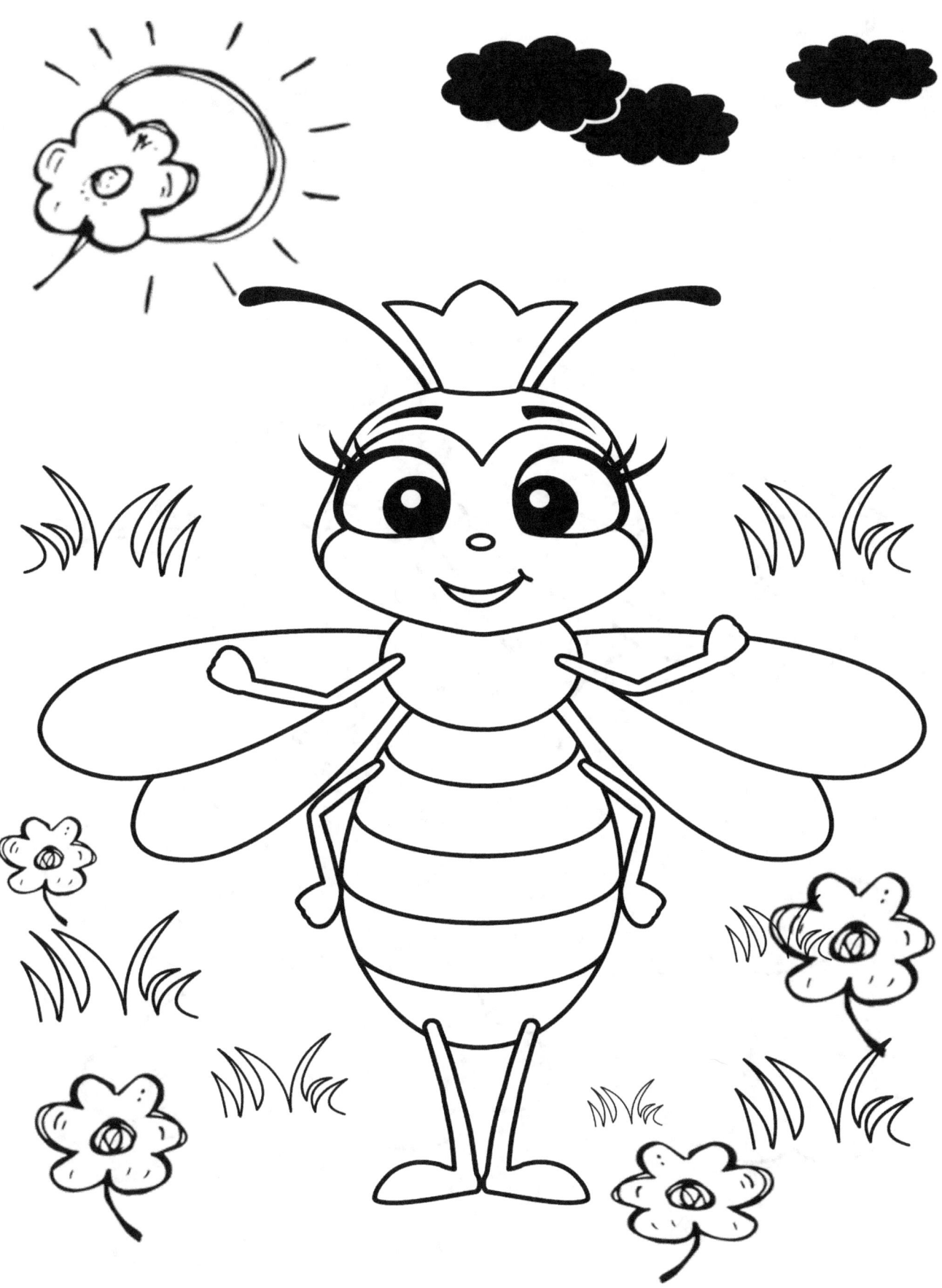

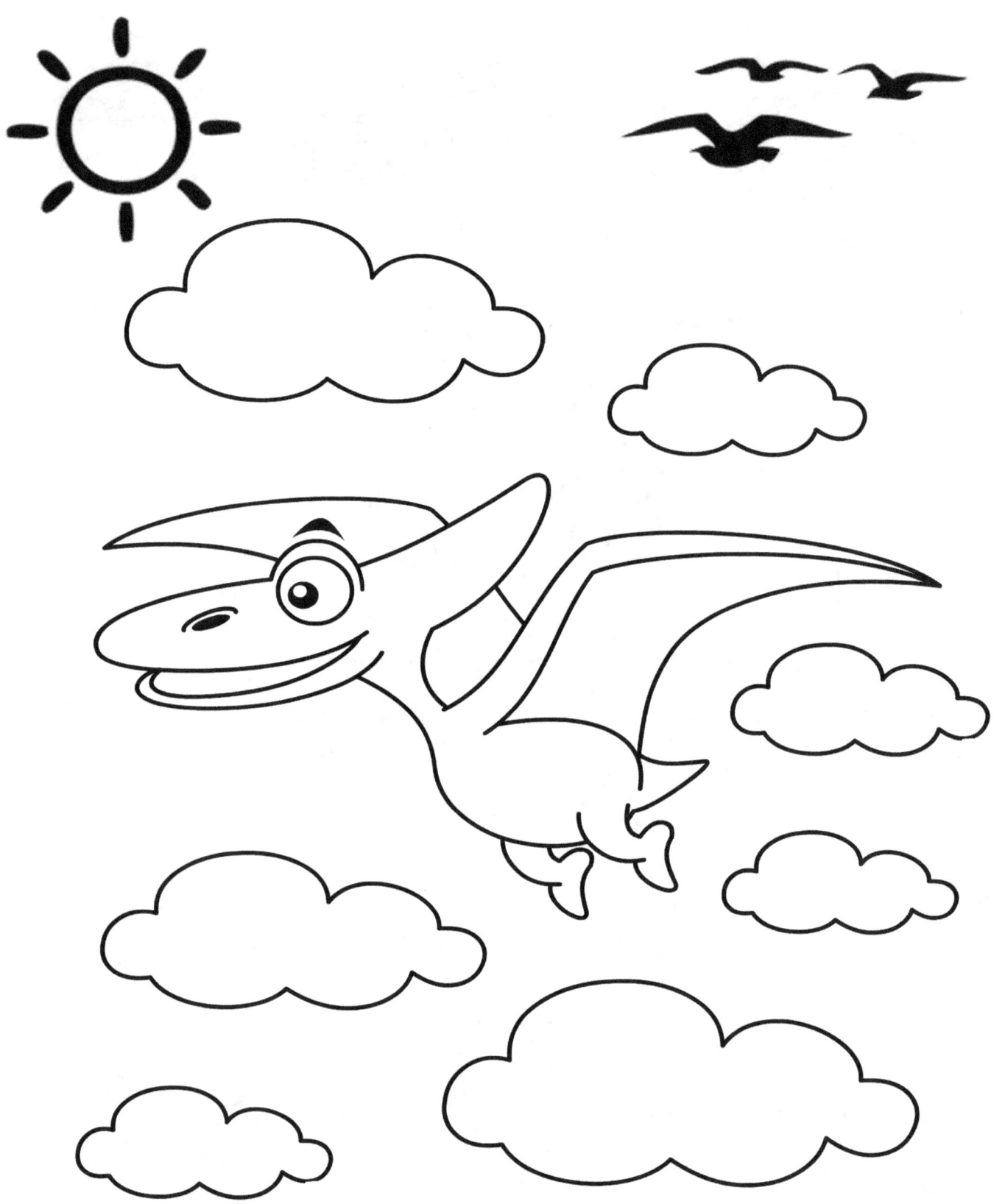

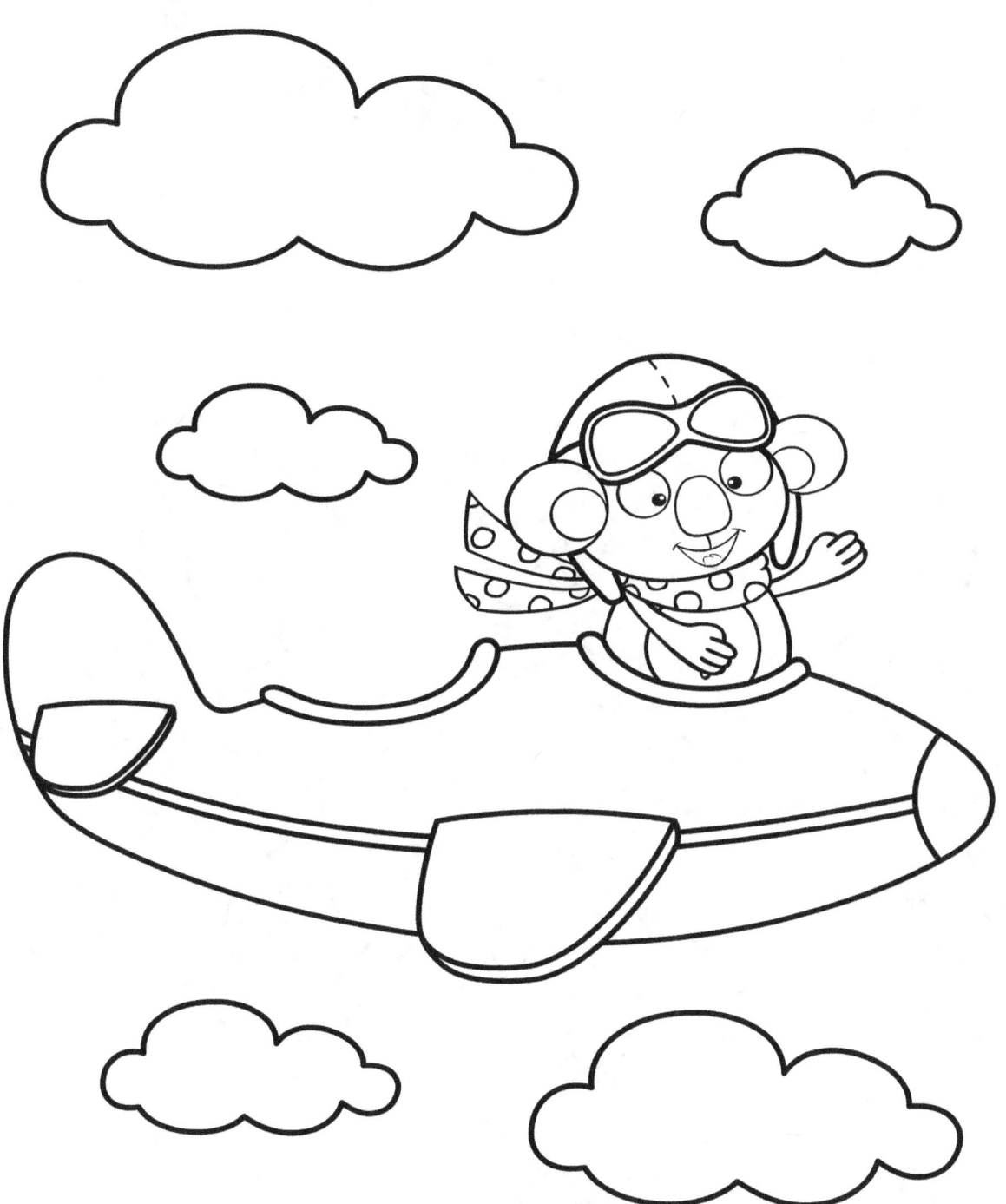

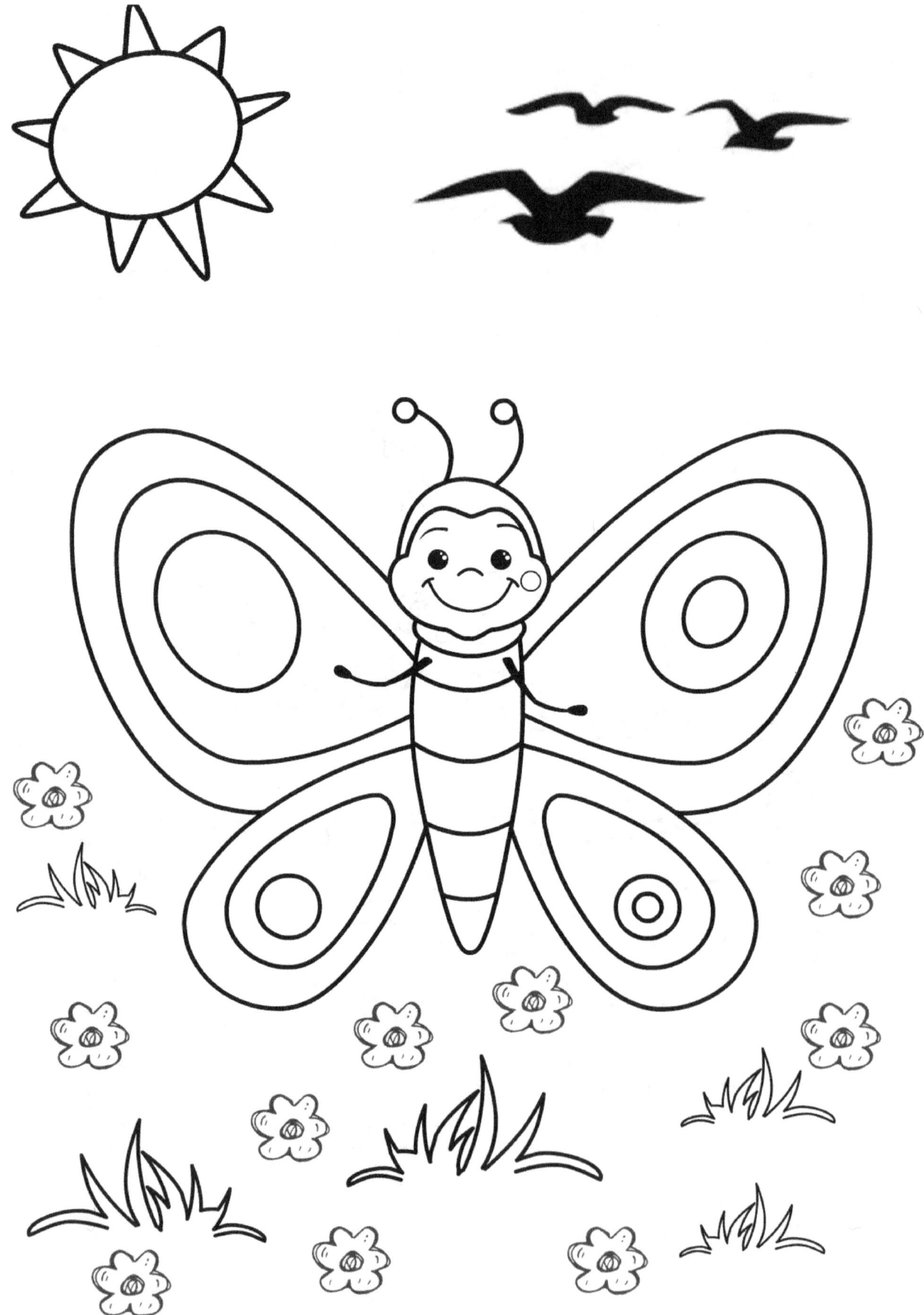

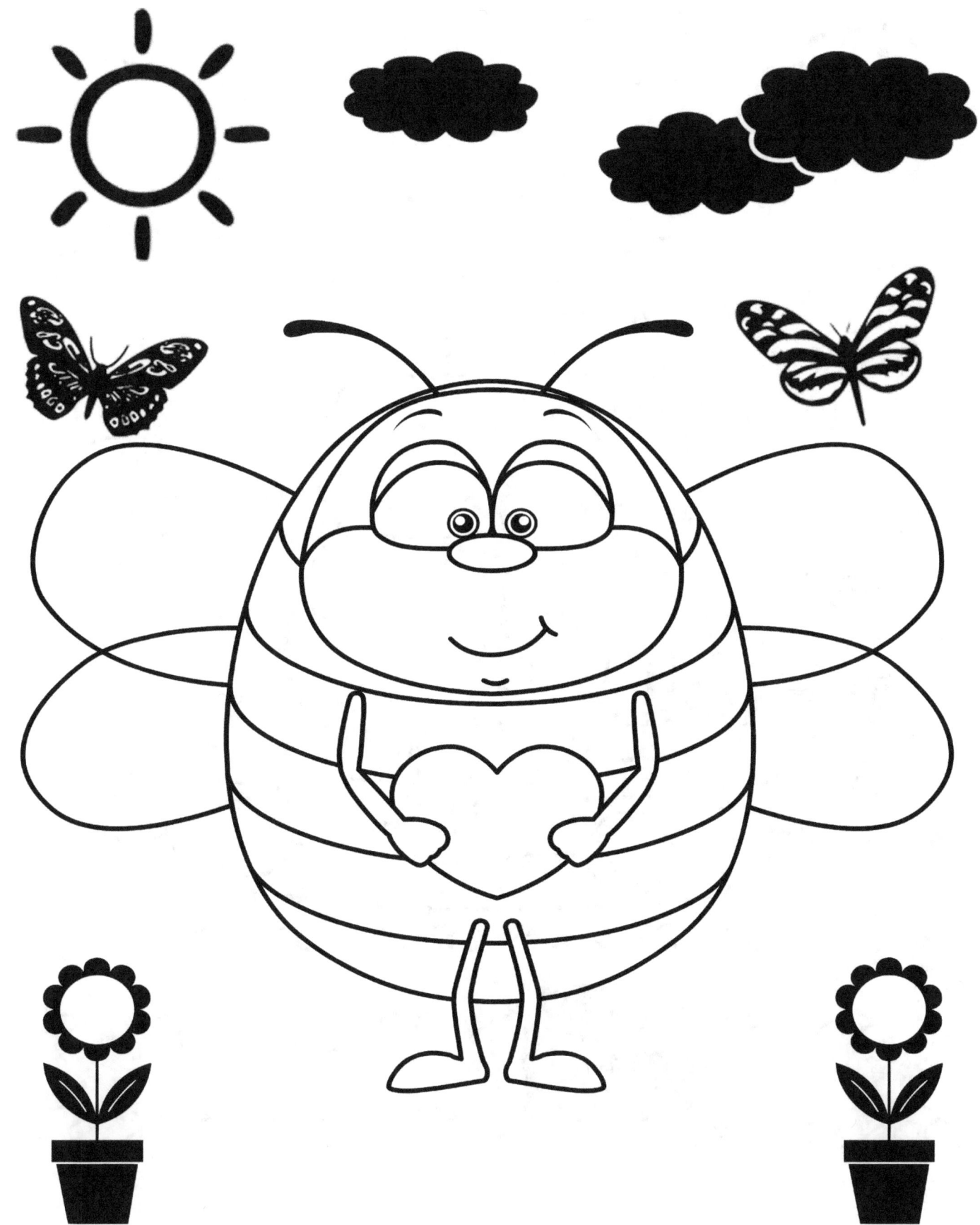

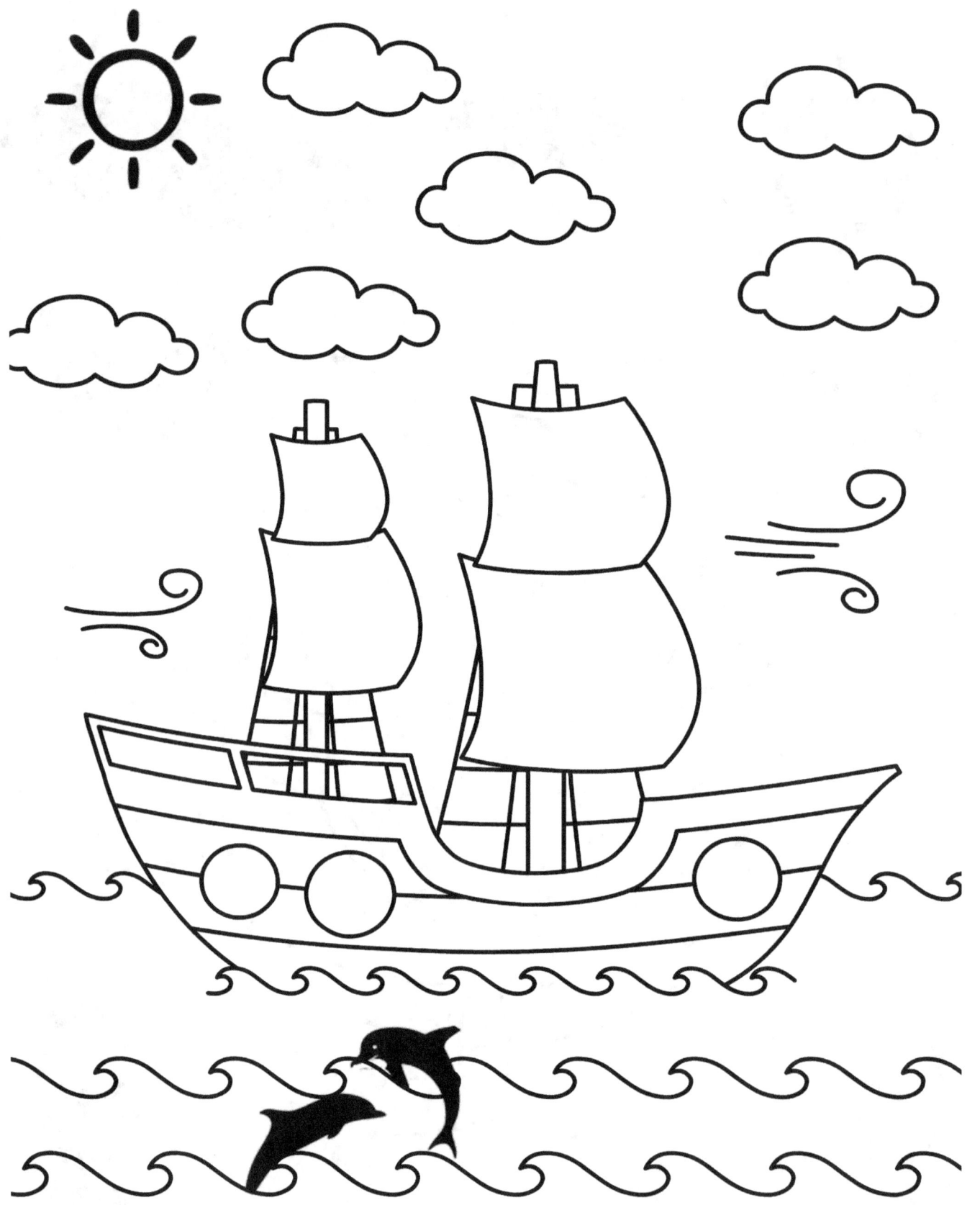

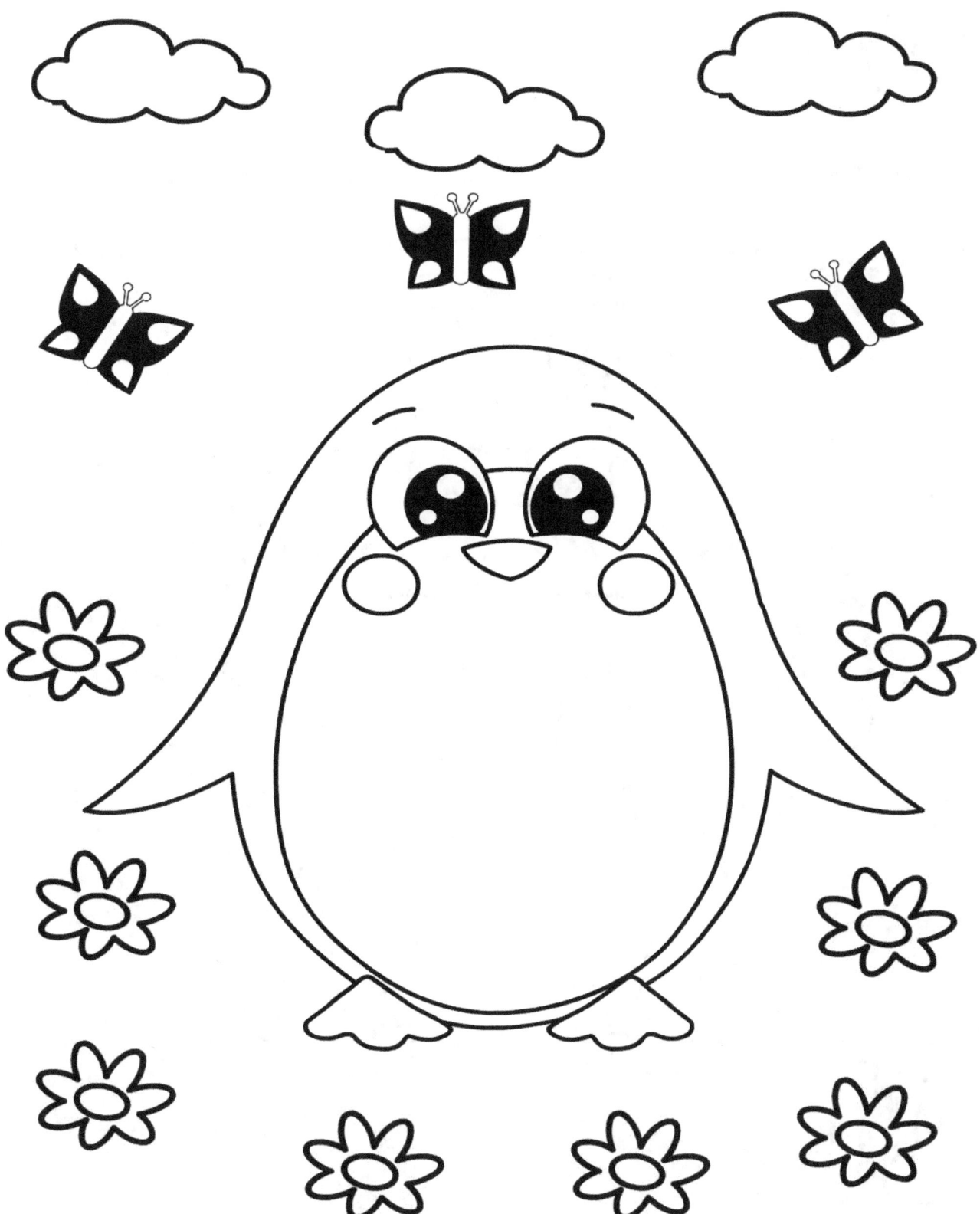

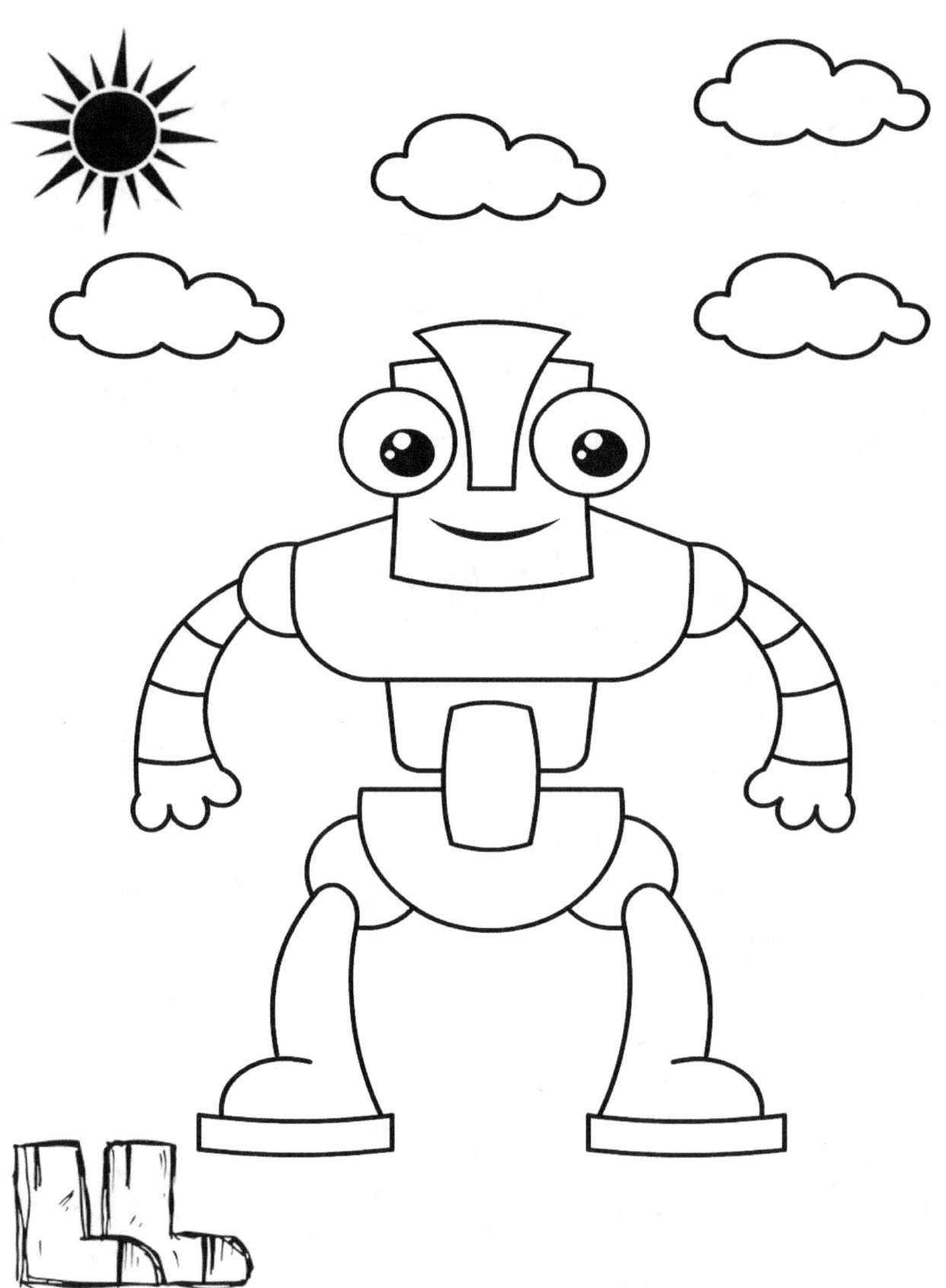

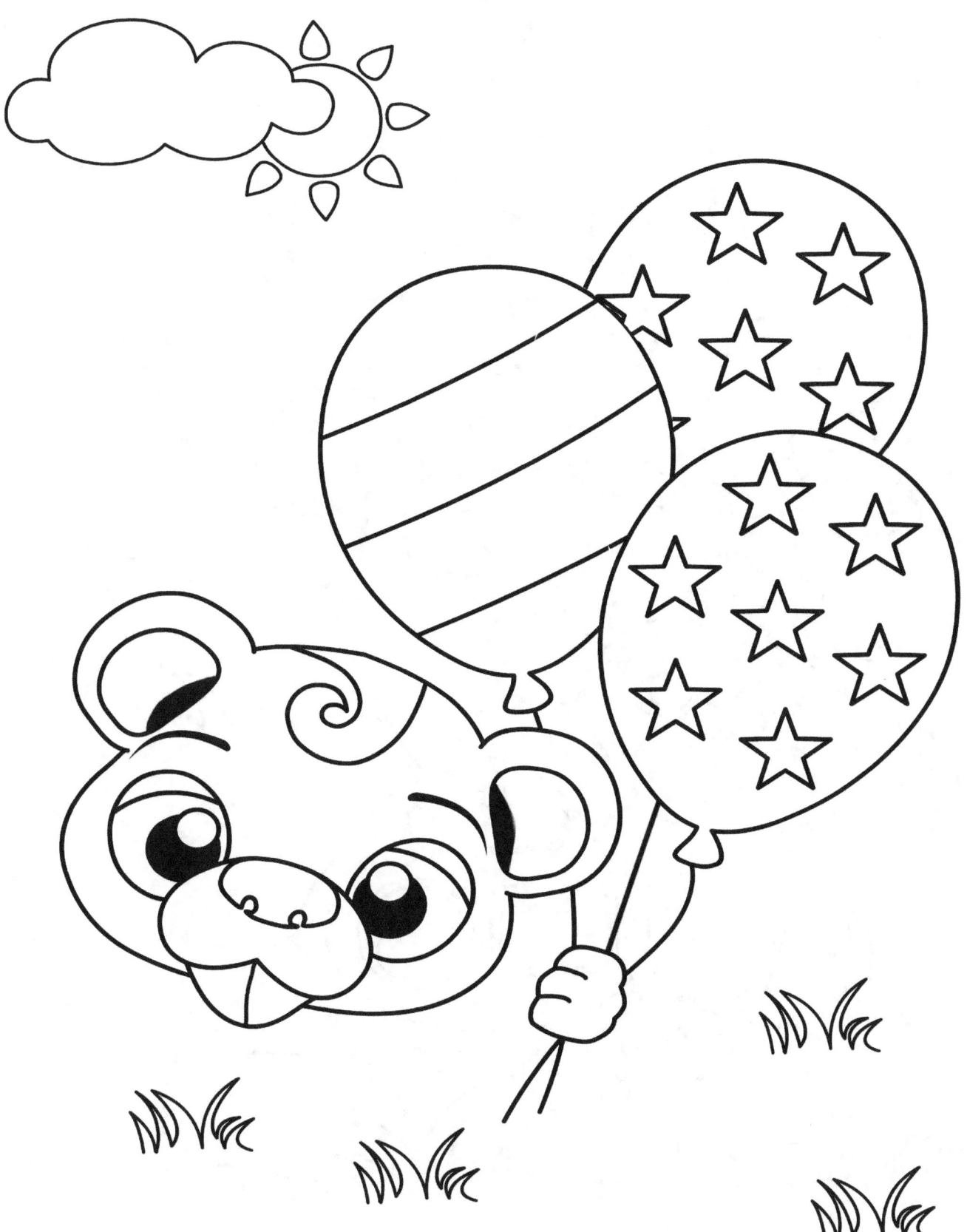

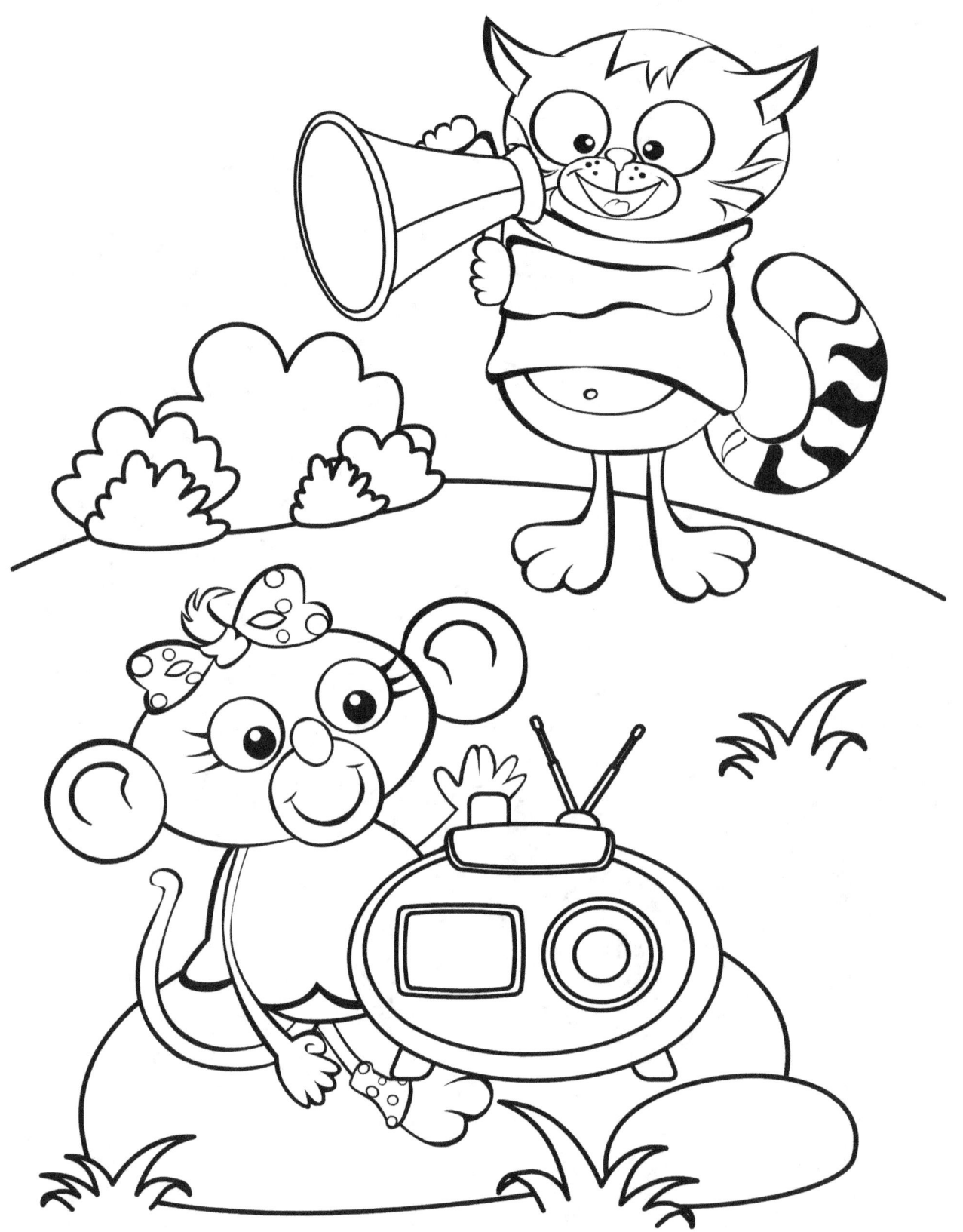

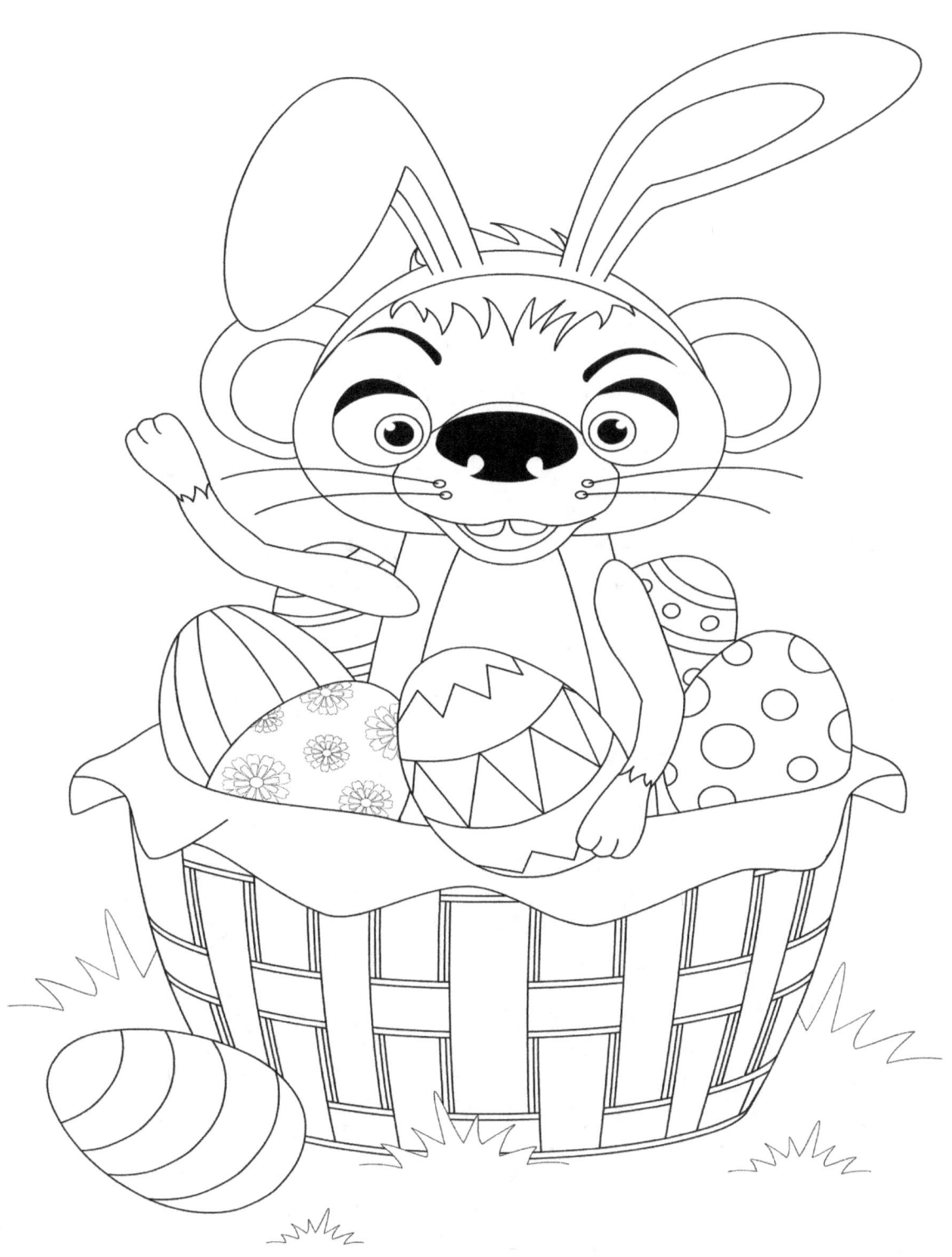

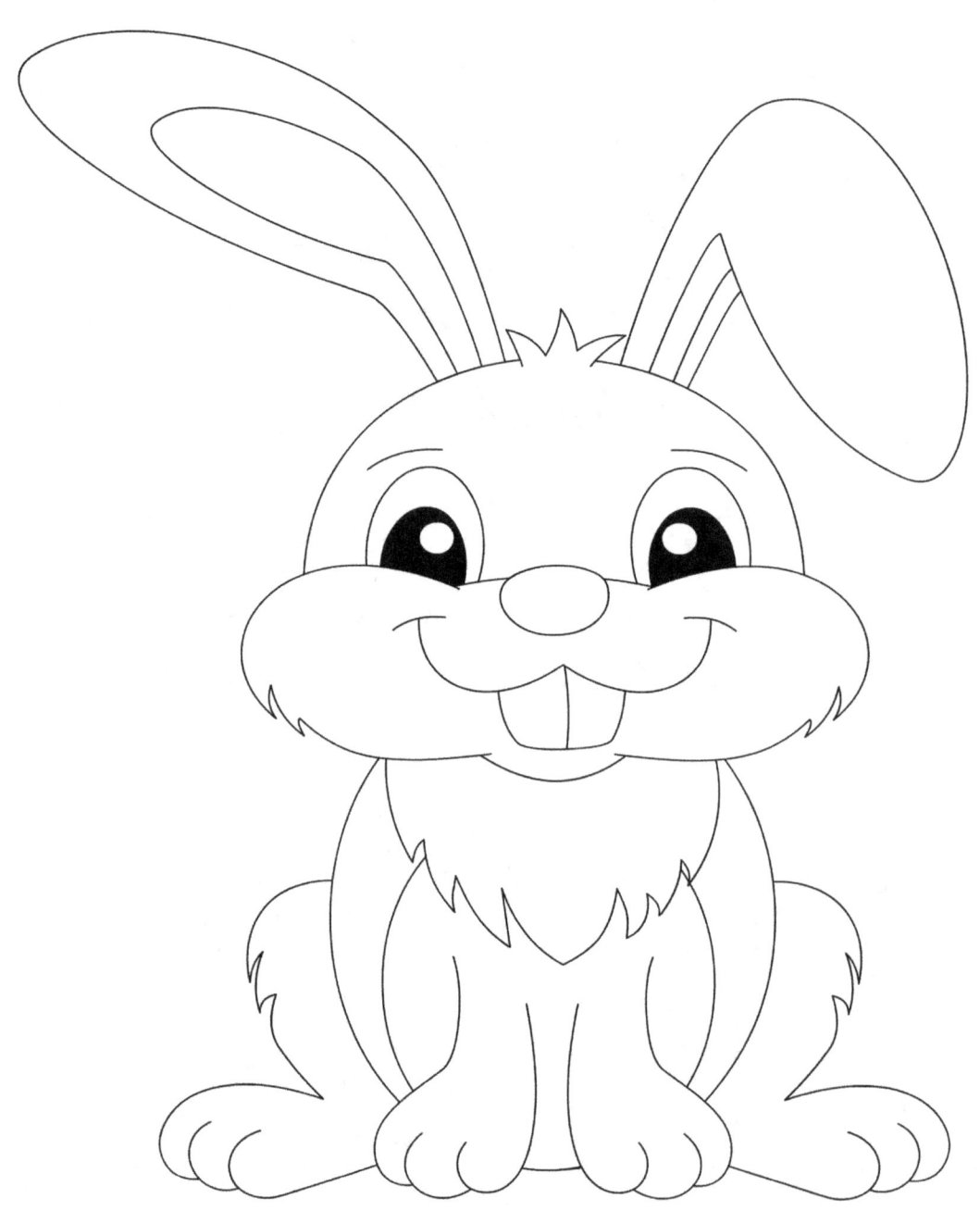

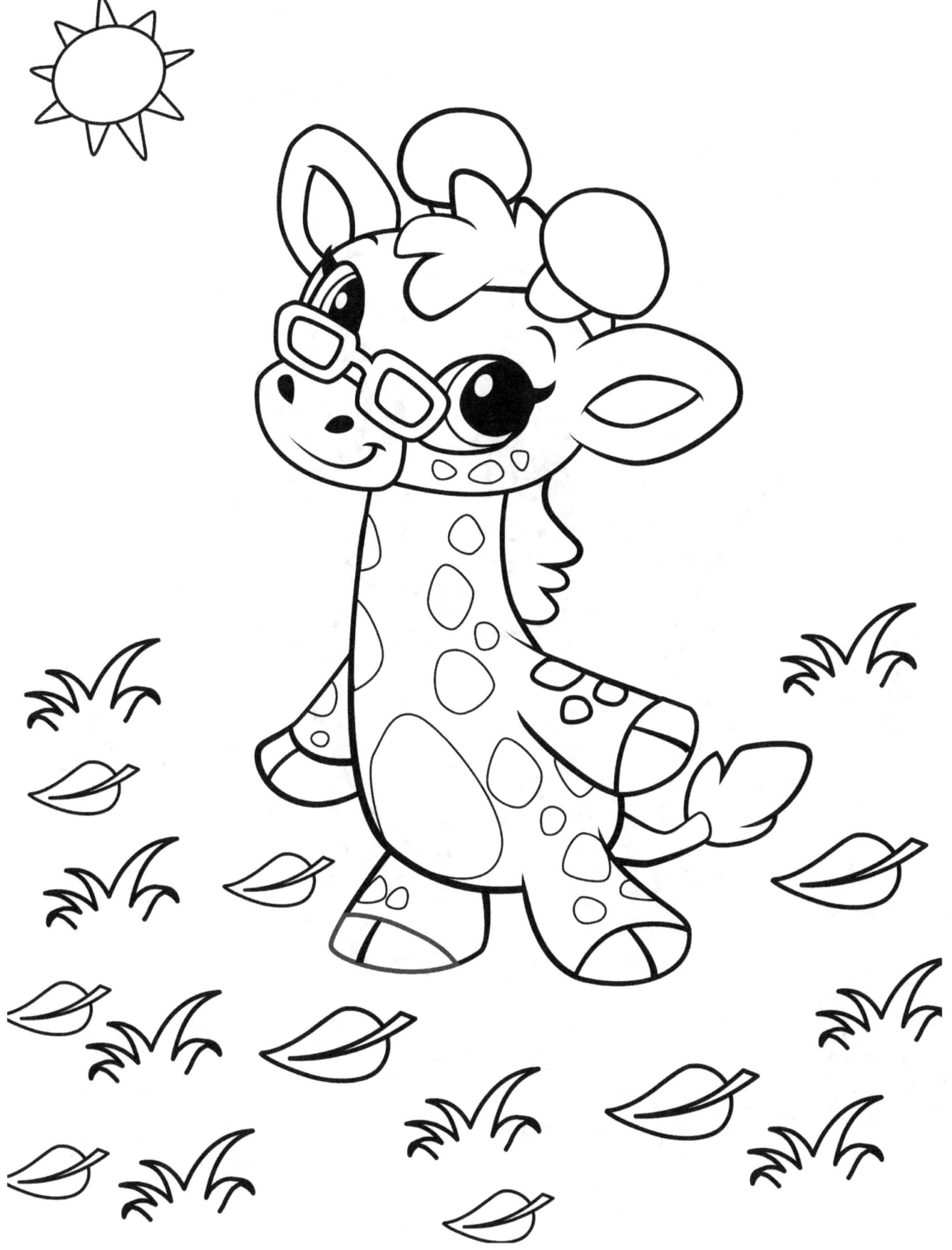

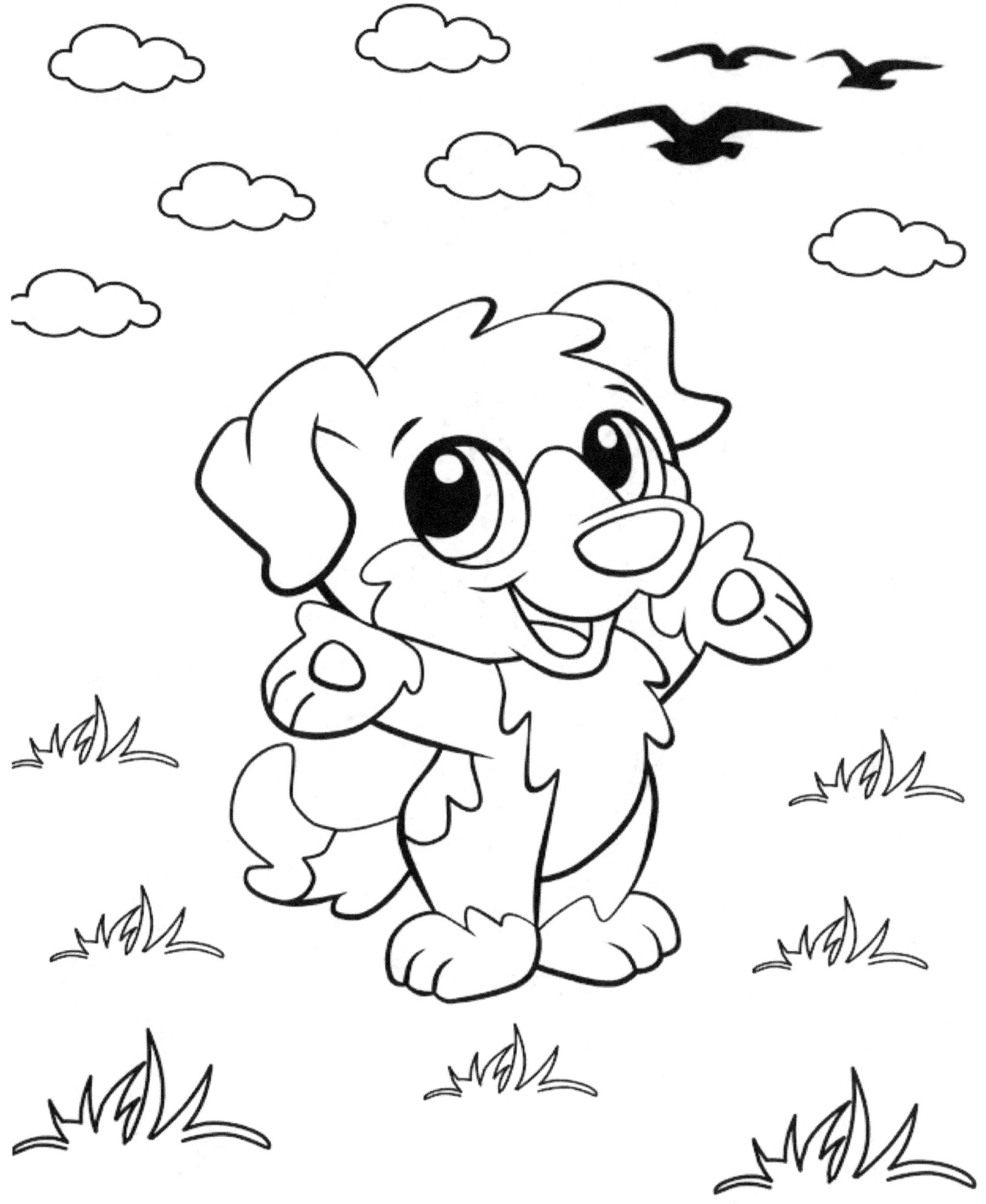

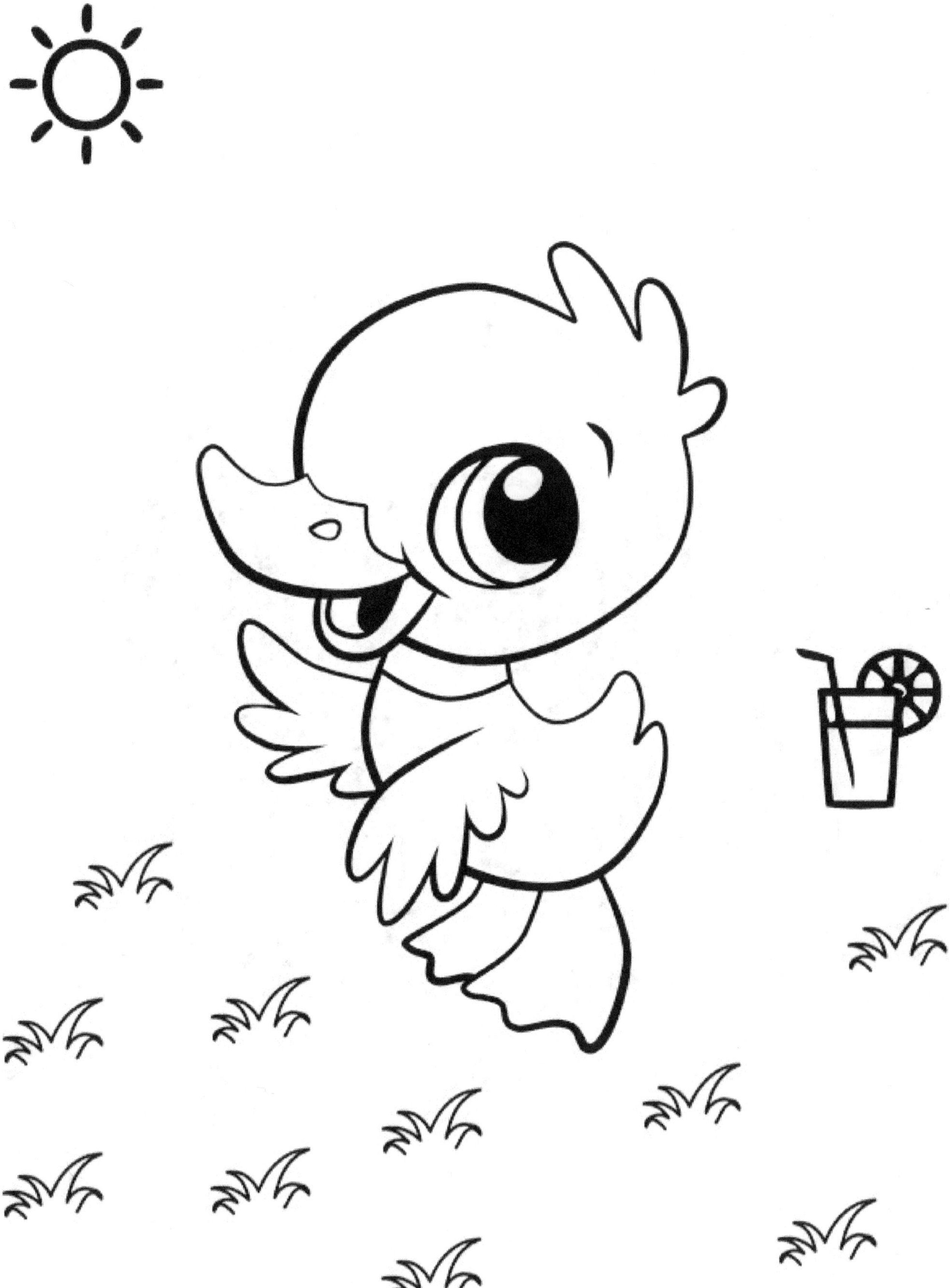

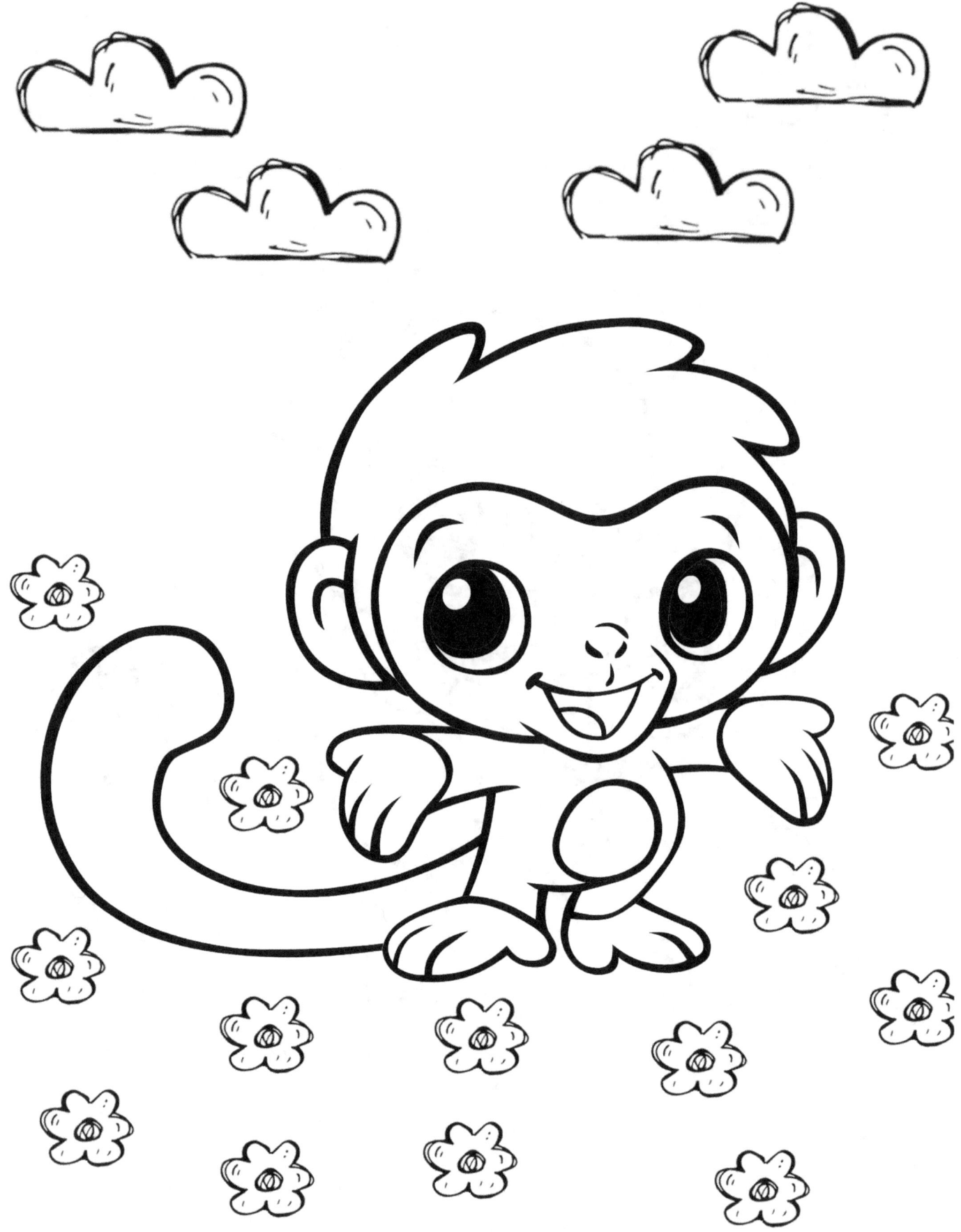

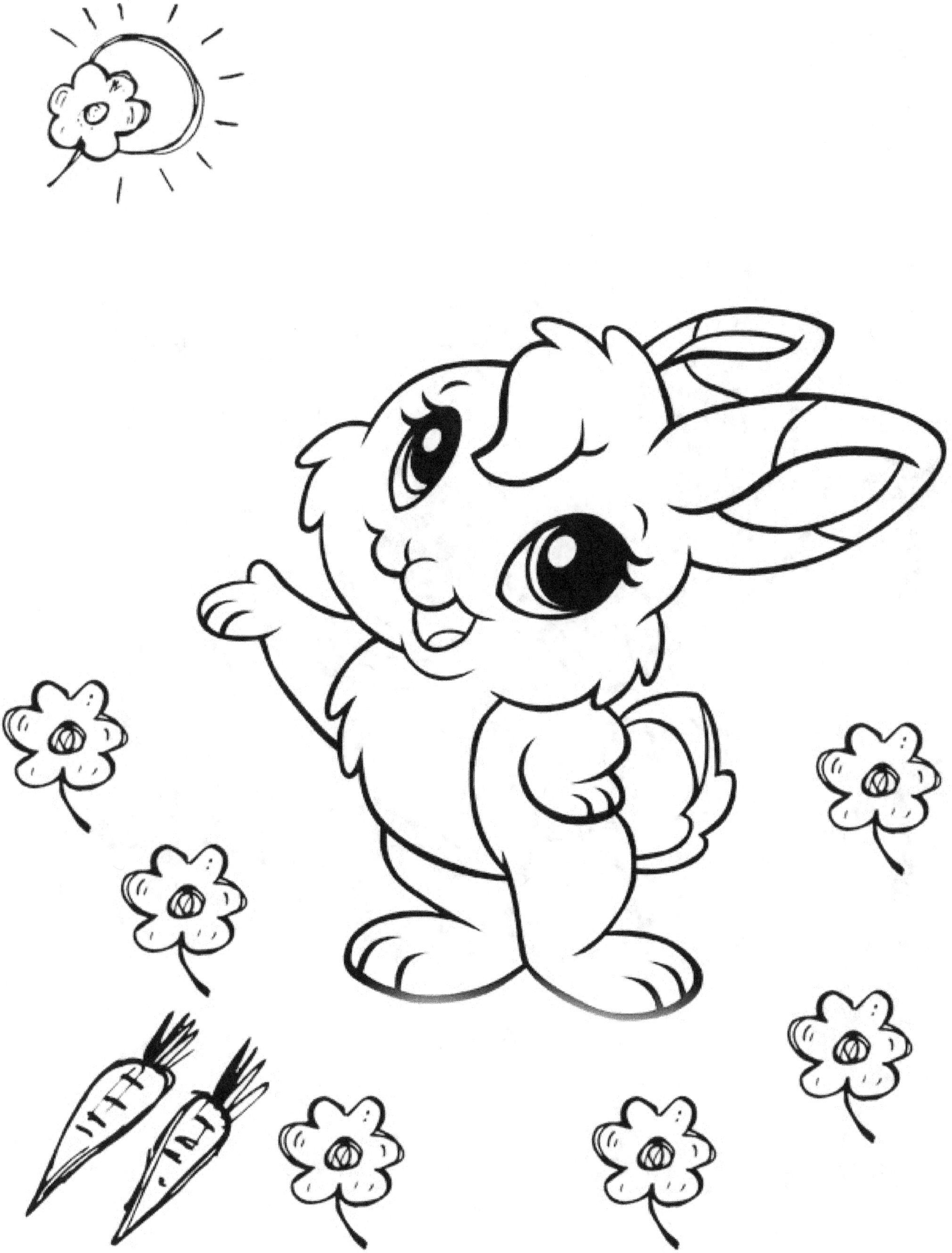

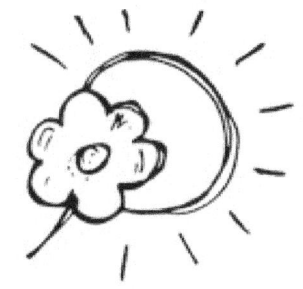

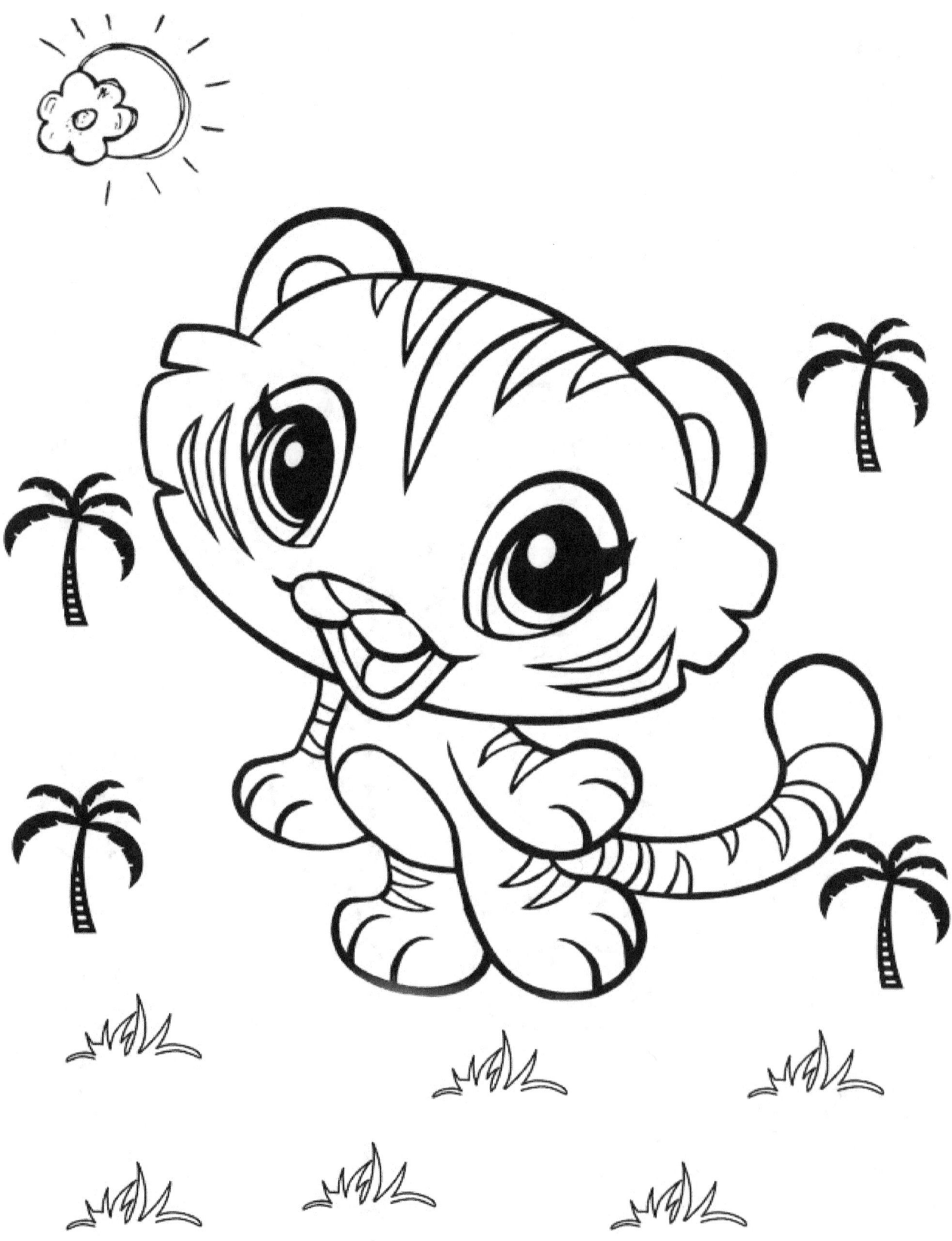

This is a page for you
Draw anything you want !
enjoy

This is a page for you
Draw anything you want !
enjoy

This is a page for you
Draw anything you want !
enjoy

This is a page for you
Draw anything you want !
enjoy

This is a page for you
Draw anything you want !
enjoy

This is a page for you
Draw anything you want !
enjoy

This is a page for you
Draw anything you want !
enjoy

This is a page for you
Draw anything you want !
enjoy

This is a page for you
Draw anything you want !
enjoy

This is a page for you
Draw anything you want !
enjoy

www.ingramcontent.com/pod-product-compliance
Lightning Source LLC
Chambersburg PA
CBHW080952220526
45465CB00008BA/3249